CRITICAL APPROACHES
VOL. 2
OSSIE ENEKWE

Edited by Gmt Emezue [Ph.D.]
Senior Lecturer, Dept. of English
Language and Literature
Ebonyi State University
Abakaliki-Nigeria

HANDEL
Library of African Writing

CRITICAL APPROACHES Vol. 2
Ossie Enekwe

Edited by GMT Emezue [Ph.D.]

Publishers:
African Books Network
Handel Books Limited
6/9 Handel Avenue
AI EBS Nigeria WA
Email: handelbook@yahoo.co.uk

© 2008. All rights reserved, which include the rights of reproduction, storage in a retrieval system, or transmission in any form by any means whether electronic or recording except as provided by International copyright law.

Marketing and Distribution in the U.S. UK,
Europe, N. America (US and Canada),
and Commonwealth countries outside Africa by
African Books Collective Ltd.
PO Box 721
Oxford OX1 9EN
Email: orders@africanbookscollective.com

ISBN:978-9-7835-0355-7

A Handel Book Publication

Visit our website at:
http://www.africaresearch.org/handelbooks/del.htm

Front and Back Cover design at *African Books Network*

Contents

0. Introduction
ONUORA OSSIE ENEKWE 7

CRITIQUES

1. Feminine Archetypes
IN OSSIE ENEKWE'S POETRY 11

2. Enekwe's Images 23

3. "Broken Pots"
THE LANGUAGE OF ENEKWE'S POETRY 47

4. Poetry and History
ENEKWE ON WAR AND DECADENCE 59

5. Shadows of Grief
THE LAST BATTLE AND OTHER STORIES 75

6. Ecocritical Spaces
NATURE IN THE NEW NIGERIAN POETRY 91

7. Post-colonial Power Tensions
IN CURRENT WEST AFRICAN POETRY 113

8. **Children's Poetry** 127
   OSSIE ENEKWE AND AGWU UDE

9. **History and Memory** 145
   ENEKWE'S MARCH TO KILIMANJARO

10. **Hope and Despair** 159
    IN ENEKWE'S *COME THUNDER*

REVIEWS

11. **A Sacred Endeavour** 173

12. **From Dream into Nightmare** 185

13. **The Marks of Carnage** 189

14. **In Demolition of the Old Dance** 195

CHAT

15. **Aesthetics of African Literature** 201
    A DISCOURSE WITH OSSIE ENEKWE

Introduction
Onuora Ossie Enekwe

This second volume of Critical Approaches is an exposition of the craft of Nigerian writer, theatre director, poet, dramatist and editor of international repute, Onuora Ossie Enekwe. The professor of dramatic literature who spent thirty years developing and advancing the drama and graduate curriculum of the University of Nigeria Nsukka had, in addition, been editor of *Okike: African Journal of New Writing* (founded by Chinua Achebe) at the university where he was also director of the Institute of African Studies.

Ossie Enekwe was born 12th November 1942 in Enugu Nigeria. He graduated 1971 from the English department of the University of Nigeria with Second Class Honours (Upper Division). After the end of nearly three years of civil war, Enekwe travelled to the United States in 1972 to complete MFA in Writing, M.Phil and Ph.D degrees in Theatre at Columbia University, New York. He was poet-in-public-service at New York, and poet-in-residence /writing fellow at other American universities.

Enekwe fought on the Biafran side in the Nigerian civil war, straddling his guitar to battle. Some chronicles of that experience abound in his books *Broken Pots* (1978) and *The Last Battle and other Stories* (1996) among others. *Marching to Kilimanjaro* (2005) and *Gentle Birds, come to me* (2007) belong to his later works. Enekwe's writing, which manipulate irony and dramatic action for aesthetic effect, have drawn some positive commentaries by readers of African literature. As an ex-soldier whom fortune had spared the death that took his kinsman and fellow poet, Chris Okigbo, in war, it is easy to understand the "unavoidably tragic" notes of his stories and the "threnodic essence" of most of his poetry which underlie the artist's sensitivity to human friendships, citizenship and nationhood. Enekwe's poetry and fiction on the war of 1968-1979 have equally thrown light on polemical issues in Nigerian writing glossed over by critics of Enekwe's own, and most of the younger, generation.

Ossie Enekwe has been the major proponent of oneness of ritual and drama. His seminal critical volumes *Igbo Masks: The Oneness of Ritual and Theatre* (1978 and *Theories of Dance in Nigeria* (1991) unravel hitherto unexplored aspects of African theatrical and dance practices. It is by such commitment of his creative and critical resources to modern criticism of African and African-American literature that Enekwe bolsters the intellectual effort of African scholars toward an indigenous aesthetics of African literature.

The proceeding chapters appraise Enekwe's craft in his works of poetry being *Broken Pots* and *Marching to Kilimanjaro* including a major reading of *The Last Battle*, an important but neglected novel on the Nigerian civil war. There are three major parts to the book. The first part, which is the longest of the three series, contains scholarly assessments of the merits and perceived drawbacks of Enekwe's poetry. Enekwe has been compared with contemporary poets from Africa like Anyidoho, Ce, Ushie and Ude. The second part deals with major reviews of Ossie Enekwe's lesser known and other popular writings while the last section features my chat with him on various subjects of literary interest.

The critical approaches in this book will widen the latitude for historical, ideological and stylistic criticism of contemporary writing in Africa in general. Some chapters have employed familiar Western theoretical platforms for the study of Enekwe's work. Hopefully future African and world literature will involve more extensive undertakings in the criticism of Enekwe's and other serious African writings of our time.

GMT   AUGUST 2008

 Critiques

1

Feminine Archetypes
IN OSSIE ENEKWE'S POETRY
C. Schneider

BARBARA Melosh in her book, *Gender and American History Since 1890*, posits that "gender" is socially constructed. Her classic example comes from Nineteenth-century Victorian culture which she notes, "described sexual difference in terms of the duties and obligations that followed from men's and women's inherent characteristics" (7). Melosh further claims that "Women's moral superiority made them ideal wives and mothers, charged with the solemn responsibility of guiding errant children and men" (7).

Many socially constructed notions have been perpetuated through the literary works and abiding philosophies of many societies. Elaine Showalter in her paper, "Towards a Feminist Poetics", is of the opinion that when we study "stereotypes of women, the sexism of male critics", and the "limited roles" women play in literary history, "we are not learning what women have felt and experienced, but what men have thought women should be" (34-

36). Hence recent Feminist interest in literary criticism is directed at exposing how ideas of gender and gender relationships are constructed and transmitted through literary works. This becomes the objective of this exercise to assess how Onuora Enekwe's portrayal of women pander to archetypal inscriptions of women as either mother (*the Madonna*) or destroyer (*la femme fatale*) – masculinist portraitures which aid in entrenching contestable notions and myths of male superiority and female inferiority. In contesting phallocentric systems of thought and dismantling logocentricism, Feminist criticism has upstaged Masculinist female (mis)perceptions and (mis)presentations while simultaneously deconstructing patriarchal "systems of thought which legitimize themselves by reference to some presence or point of authority prior to and outside of themselves" (Hawthorn 130).

The image and personality of women in Enekwe's oeuvres easily come across with a critical view of some poems in Enekwe's three collections – *Broken Pots* (published in 1977), *Marching to Kilimanjaro* (published in 2005) and *Gentle Birds Come to me* (published in 2007). These supposedly evidence the poet's concern for women and their well being. However the poet perceives and subsequently inscribes women as what Selden and Widdowson term "beings of subjectivity" (189). Throughout Enekwe's poetry, two major archetypes are purveyed of women: Women as destroyers, the femme fatale, and women as mothers, the Madonna-and-child. In much of poetry, as in other genres, literary archetypes, being "recurrent narrative designs, patterns of action, character types or images identifiable in a wide variety of works of literature, as well as myths", are usually held to reflect "a set of universal, primitive and elemental mental forms or patterns whose effective embodiment in a literary work evoke a profound response from the reader" (Abrams 224). In thus appraising and challenging some feminine archetypes in

African literature such as Enekwe's poetry, it will be seen that readers may be led into holding erroneous conjectures that subtly impact upon their assessment of womanhood. Instances of this misplacement of ideas are obvious from Enekwe's constructs which serve to undermine femaleness and perpetuate the stereotype of her as a being of simple qualities. No doubt both ideas are borne out of male phallocentric and masculinist attempts to culturally dominate and relegate women to subservient positions the world over.

THE FEMME FATALE

In discussing archetypal femme fatale image constructed in Enekwe's poetry, we turn to the poems, "Lady Death" (*Broken Pots*) and "Prayer for Peace" (*Marching to Kilimamjaro*) as typical examples. Although both poems are published in different anthologies by Enekwe – in fact, the latter is published twenty eight years after the former – yet we see the poet exploring the same notion of women in both poems.

In "Lady Death" the destructive woman of Shaw's imagining is reflected through the image of a female praying mantis whose actions are reported by the male "voice". It begins with a sarcastic comment on the idea of love between man and woman: "Love can be a dangerous game", he observes. Where or how this danger originates is not clear. The next line never takes us to any raison d'etre for this overture between man and woman in love (referred to here as "Mantis" and "his lady"). By refusing to provide some explanatory details as a signpost of a "love game", the poet insults our intelligence. However, what follows is even more disturbing as the poetic voice describes a macabre "love-death" ritual:

> in the region of terrible heat
> she clasps him within her thighs

> ensconces his head between her teeth
> and with the swiftness of guillotine blade
> chops it off… (*Pots* 30)

Now we are provided the persona's own simplistic, if not prosaic, explanation for the murderous instinct of the female species:

> so the dance can endure
> without remorse or wasteful introspection. (30)

No doubt this succeeds more in establishing the wickedness of the perpetrator of the action rather than explicating the situations that give rise to it. By this Enekwe condemns the woman for heinous crimes and sentences her to states of criminality, irrationality and stupidity. It is similar to Jane Tompkins' observations on the movie *Gunfight at the OK Corral* where two characters Doc Halliday and Jo Van Fleet star as degraded characters. Tompkins remarks that

> Doc Holliday is a similarly degraded character. He used to be a dentist and is now a gambler who lives to get other people's money away from them; he is a drunk, and he abuses the woman that loves him. But his weaknesses, in the perspective of the movie, are glamorous. He is irresistible, charming, seductive, handsome, witty, commanding. … The degradation doesn't stick to (him) … it is all absorbed by his female counterpart, the 'slut', Jo Van Fleet. (136)

The chauvinistic portrayal of woman as seen above, and which Enekwe attempts in his poetry, serves to undermine the integrity of women as rational beings while simultaneously establishing them as extremely ruinous and self serving species with killer instincts. Hence like the projection of Jo Van Fleet in the movie, any time we encounter Enekwe's archetypal woman, "we are embarrassed every time she appears on the screen, because every time, she is humiliated further" (136). Such notions of female irrationality and invisibility as offered by Enekwe in his poetry find explication in a Nigerian critic's expose about women of Yorubaland whose culture has made it such that

> women are 'naturally' excluded from public affairs; they are viewed as unable to hold positions of responsibility, rule men or even be visible when serious matters of state and society are being discussed. Women are viewed to need tutelage before they can be politically active... (Ogundipe-Leslie 130)

In the poem "Prayer for Peace" Enekwe's recourse to his cherished masculinist theme is done with a touch of irony where men are presented as innocent victims (and acolytes) at the "altar" of feminine abuse. Hence they resort to "prayer" to deflect the evil of femininity. Once again, the subject matter here, sex, is seen to wield a disastrous outcome on humanity. Employing a Hellenistic metaphor (Troy), Enekwe evokes scenes of destruction and disaster unleashed on "bewildered children crying to heaven" and wretched "widow(s) in black" who join the "funeral train" to the place of burials. The cause for such grand destructions, we are told, lies in the mythical powers of the sexual organ, as symbolized by the "lifted thigh". Here female sexuality is misprised as wreaking only havoc and destructive violence on society. The "thigh" is of quasi religious power and significance and thus assumes the image and instrument of disaster:

> your lifted thigh
> deflects the planets
> disturbs the seas

floods farmlands. (31)

Woman's ability to destroy man throughout the ages, as the poem suggests, is entrenched in her sexuality which the poet further vulgarizes thus:

> ...the corrosive liquid of passion,
> the pulverization of flesh
> in the intensity of copulation. (31)

This supposed power of woman over man can only be calmed with prayers, ubiquitous sacrifices and supplications as suggested in the last stanza of the poem:

> Queen of fire
> be steady and calm
> ...
> open to peace the gates of the city. (32)

Here the poet entrenches the notion of male rational balance by resorting to the myth of an opposing irrational female power. The poet's dilemma here is similar to Bishop's in "The Fish" which Patricia Yaeger rationalizes as the dilemma of killing "the object" in order to "assert the subject." As she comments,

> the question in other words, is how one writes poetry about an "other", who has an extra-human power the self thinks it needs, without destroying that other's alienness. Should the poet kill the fish, eat him, absorb him? If she refuses she may relinquish the possibility of internalizing this venerability and relinquish as well the enactment of a ritual moment of empowerment, of making

herself greater than she was before by absorbing his *tremendum*. (195)

However Enekwe, unlike Bishop, does not have to kill his "Helen" physically in order to internalize her "*tremendum*". He redirects his quest into quasi religious realms where ultimately the object (woman) is supposedly conquered (calmed) by her worshipful acolytes. Thus it is still a woeful tale of subjugation and abuse, cleverly crafted in lyrics of admiring denouncements prior to the final conquest. Hence under thorough investigation, such powers as suggested by the poet (all lost in the mist of myths) do not actually exist.

THE MADONNA

This is one other portraiture of woman in Enekwe's poetry using the Madonna image where women are only seen and heard through her power and ability to nurture and protect their children. It is ubiquitously sustained in poetry of Africa of pre-independence and post-colonial periods by Diop and Senghor. The archetypal mother-and-child is readable in the following poems of Enekwe: "To Mother on her birthday" (*Broken Pots*), "Black woman" (*Marching to Kilimanjaro*), "That I could fly" and "Nneka" (*Gentle Birds Come to me*).

In "To Mother on her Birthday," Enekwe begins his stereotype of woman as a nurturing self sacrificing and long suffering symbol. In the first stanza, the poet seeks to establish the reason for this relationship:

> ... you did more
> than bring us into the world
> and let us suck life

> from your nipples. (11)

Maternal duty is offered as the raison d'etre for the survival of feminine identity. Here she must be stable and self-effacing. Maternal love is "a love that thrives like Iroko" (*Pots* 12) in its all embracing nature. Mother's voice is "beautiful as dawn" and "...sweet as songs woven by black birds among sunflowers" (*Gentle* 38) because she "nurtured and tended" her children. Her tender care gives the suckling baby

> sweet sensations (that) rise in pressure
> Tiny legs kick with pleasure
> Sleep comes gently and strong
> Sleep whispers softly and long. (9)

Her self-sacrificing nature is observed through her understanding that

> ... to love her baby
> is to bathe her and wipe
> her nostrils, mouth and rump. ("Mother" *Pot* 12)

As Mother she knows it is her duty to caution and sympathize:

> My child, you may rove
> to discover the world
> but do not follow everything
> that pleases your eyes. ("Fly" *Gentle* 38)

And for the poet, as for Okonkwo's uncle in the classic African novel *Things Fall Apart* by Chinua Achebe, "Mother is supreme."

Outside of these roles the mothering woman does not have an

identity of her own. As Tompkins opines, women are "used as extensions of men, mirrors of men, devices for showing men off, devices for helping men get what they want. They are never there in their own right, or rarely...." (136). In this instance, as Enekwe suggests, women get recognized as a result of their role as mothers. Once this dubious stamp is removed or deflated, we may assume that the woman ceases to exist. To Enekwe, the ideal woman is a symbol of nurture (or perhaps self-torture and self-annihilation) which equates succor, endurance, self-sacrifice, patience, tolerance, wisdom, hard work and suffering. This steadfast love and stoicism of a suffering woman is likened to Africa which the poet refers to as "Queen of perpetual smile /and gentle, flowing sadness" and one whose "warm breasts/ light the corridors of life" (*Kilimanjaro* 29)

In line with this image of African womanhood, fostered in the tradition of leading Francophone poets like Leopold Senghor, Africa was to endure and forgive its colonial rape and degradation and, moreover, is expected to continue this endurance with such long suffering platitudes that Enekwe offers. But as Mariama Ba cited in Schipper opines, "we no longer accept the nostalgic praise to the African mother who, in his anxiety, man confuses with mother Africa" (47). Obviously Enekwe's perception of womanhood betrays this element of anxiety that Ba had suggested. Thus there is need for cultural sensitization which will overhaul such idealization and romanticisation of African womanhood because, as Florence Stratton observes, "through the Mother Africa trope, they (men) mask the subordination of women in the patriarchal socio-political systems of African states from which they do, indeed, need to be liberated" (55). Patricia Waugh opines of this subjectivization that

> once women have experienced themselves as 'subjects' then they can begin to problematize and to deconstruct the socially constructed subject positions available to them, and to recognize

that an inversion of the valuation of 'maleness' and 'femaleness' will not in itself undermine the social construction of masculinity and feminity. (25)

There is need to project women in all entirety as literary subjects with human complexities that men are endowed with. Enekwe's projection of feminine archetypes may have just succeed in perpetuating myths that subjugate and undermine womanhood but, as has been attempted by Chinua Achebe and Ngugi wa Thiong'o in their more recent works, male writers must overhaul the limited portraiture of their women, and of womanhood, so as to reconstruct and create a more positive visioning of womanhood in the literature of modern Africa.

WORKS CITED

Abrams, M.H *Glossary of Literary Terms*. Orlando: Harcourt Brace Jovanovich, 1993.

Melosh, Barbara. *Gender and American History since 1890*. London: Routledge, 1993.

Ogundipe-Leslie, Omolara. "African women, culture and another Development." *Presence Africaine*. 1987, 141:1 123-39.

Rice, Philip and Patricia Waugh eds. *Modern Literary Theory: A Reader*. London: Arnold, 1996.

Rubin, Gayle. "The Traffic of Women." *Toward an Anthropology of Women*. Ed. Rayna Rapp Reiter. New York: Ren, 1975.

Schipper, Mineke. "Mother Africa on a Pedestal: The Male Heritage in African literature and Criticism." *African Literature Today*. 1987, 15:35-54.

Selden, Raman and Peter Widdowson. *A Reader's Guide to Contemporary*

Literary Theory. Kentucky: The University Press of Kentucky, 1993.

Showalter, Elaine. "Towards a Feminist Poetics." *Women Writing About Women.* Ed. M. Jacobus. London: Croomhelm 1979.

Stratton, Florence. *Contemporary African Literature and the Politics of Gender.* London: Routledge, 1994.

Tompkins, Jane. "Me and my Shadow." *Gender and Theory: Dialogues on Feminist Criticism.* Ed Linda Kauffman. Oxford: Basil Blackwell Inc, 1989.

Yaeger, Patricia. "Toward a Female Sublime." *Gender and Theory: Dialogues on Feminist Criticism.* Ed. Linda Kauffman. Oxford: Basil Blackwell Inc, 1989.

2

Enekwe's Images

GMT Emezue

THIS chapter explores some dominant images employed by the Nigerian poet, Onuora Ossie Enekwe, in his three volumes namely, *Broken Pots* (1977), *Marching to Kilimanjaro* (2005) and *Gentle Birds Come to me* (2007). It is hoped that an outline of the dominant images in Enekwe's poems will yield deeper levels of meaning and new perspectives to the work of this African writer in the same way that Caroline Spurgeon and G. Wilson Knight, among others, had illuminated the prodigious vision of Shakespeare in their study of the English playwright.

Our term and use of "image" in this study border on a most basic definition of the word offered by M. H. Abrams as that which is used to signify "all the objects and qualities of sense perception referred to in a poem or other work of literature, whether by literal description, by allusions, or in the vehicles (secondary references) of its similes and metaphors" (86). We shall however include descriptors that have capability of communicating touch, smell, taste, sight and hearing. In this broad category, adjectival, verbal and adverbial phrases, in addition to other grammatical descriptions that communicate or convey analogies, will be part of our investigation. Spurgeon's idea of "images" incorporates these and more perhaps. To her, an "image" is a word, phrase, clause, sentence (sometimes even a whole poem) used by a poet or prose writer which can

> ... illustrate, illuminate and embellish his thought. It is a description or an idea, which by comparison or analogy stated or understood with something else, transmits to us through the emotion and associations it arouses, something of the "wholeness" the depth and richness of the way the writer views, conceives or has felt about what he is telling us. (9)

These assumptions will of course rest on whether the objects of study can be analogous, in which sense the "image", because of its evocative ability, can "create atmosphere and convey emotion in a way no precise description however clear and accurate can possibly do" (9). It was the New Critics who, early in the quarter of the twentieth century, explained the term as "implicit interaction of imagery only within a text", and which was studied as "the way that the subject and theme worked itself out in many plays, poems and novels " (Abrams 87). This view, of course, connotes an exclusivist "word-oriented" approach championed by Russian Formalists, furthered in Structuralist "geometry" of binary patterns, and perfected in Deconstructionist "decentering" of terms. Nevertheless our aim here shall be to seek meaning and interpretation of Enekwe based on images vis-à-vis author, material and human environment (which of course includes the perceived and non-perceived audience).

This investigation also relies upon the conventions of art and its function in an African society. In the words of Zulu Sofola – also espoused in other ways by Chinua Achebe, Wole Soyinka, Masizi

Kunene and Kofi Awoonor – art is

> The medium through which the soul of man reaches out beyond itself to transform and make intelligible the proddings within the inner recesses for the ultimate Truth, the meaning of existence, man's place in the cosmos, his relationship to Supreme Creator and to his fellow creatures, and finally the ultimate end of man. (2)

Sofola had gone further to outline some qualities which a true Artist ("Omata-madu") must possess since he/she "…occupies a vital place in the life of his community as a mediator between his people and their divine reality, and as a motivator for the well-being of his people" (7). The Artist in Africa, she rightly notes,

> was expected to possess a purity of soul in thought, moral sensitivity and bearing, strong spiritual connection with the Supreme Creative Force, and possessing knowledge and talent, such that his creative essence, *Ononu-Nka*, may be disturbed by the ill-health in the human condition enough to ignite his creative genius for a creation that will better the human condition, improve man's understanding of human destiny, and help evolve a better quality of human beings. (10)

The modern African poet is similarly placed by the peculiar historical and environmental circumstances of his existence to improve human understanding of the universal scheme through the range of images or out-picturing within his grasp and learning. As Spurgeon rightly avers,

> a poet will in the long run, naturally tend to draw the large proportion of his images from the objects he knows best, or thinks most about, or from the incidents among myriads he has experienced, to which he is sensitive and which therefore remain

within his knowledge. (12)

This process of communicating experiences validates the dialogic approach to literary interpretation which recognises the fundamental relationship between text, author and society. Here in these poems some of the images that Enekwe deploys reveal his awareness of the sacred role of an artist, his commitment being informed by a quest to better his society by correcting the disequilibrium which he identifies in it. For instance, while *Gentle Birds, come to me* (2007) might be a summation of the positive values envisioned by the poetic imagination, his earlier collections, *Broken Pots* (1977) and *Marching to Kilimanjaro* (2005), reflect the gross imbalance and disorder from what he shows to be a spiritual sterility that goads men on the course of violence against their fellows. This violence takes the form of the Biafran war foisted by Western imperialism with its fracture of the colonised victims (as seen in Zaire, Congo, Zimbabwe, South Africa and a host of other African nations). While it is not our purpose to investigate these recurrent historical themes (which is the fitting subject of a subsequent review), the present exercise will show how history's disruptions and imbalance are reappraised by the Nigerian poet through powerful visual picturing which enlarges the entire disorientation of the African universe in the reader's mind.

Thus Ossie Enekwe's style and method of forming images are quite peculiar; they substantiate the view that a truly good writer has "a certain range of images which are characteristic of him" (Spurgeon 13) and it is our premise that Enekwe's poetry also has a marked tendency to use these images and their associated ideas to provide larger signposts to his vision of Africa and the world.

I) HEAVENLY BODIES

Heavenly bodies like stars, comets, earth, etc., feature rather frequently in Enekwe's poetry. While some of the references are positive, others appear contrariwise. Interestingly throughout his poetry, the poet is consistent in the use of these images and the ideas they suggest:

"Comets"

References to "comets" in Enekwe's poetry suggest brief but flashy existence. This image usually has a negative association. In all instances where this analogy is made, it communicates this same sense of regret: "My generation passes away/ like comets in the gloom" (*Pots* 28);

> The hero is a comet flash
> arrow shot over dim tent
> beauty in expiration. (16)

"Mars"

The image of the planet Mars in the poem "Manhattan" is in its astrological connotation as the forebear of ancient Rome. This image of the warlike empire and its ruling planet is evident in the lines: "your men true sons of Mars/ are of copper and bronze made" (*Pots* 36).

"Moon"

In Enekwe's poetry the moon is perceived as a passive reflector: something appealing but rather short-lived. It has little power of sustenance which is always in contrast to the sun. In many places where the poet uses "moon" this has connotations of passivity as in the lines: "though our gift of blind hope bids us dream/ of moonlights dappled with stars" (*Pots* 32); "before the death of the Moon" (19); "your moon beautiful on high/ turns into a smouldering oak" (36);

    the moon redolent with roses
    pours her laughter into a cup of blood.
    (*Kilimanjaro* 56)

II) WEATHER AND ELEMENTS

Weather and other elements are frequent in Enekwe's poetry. Details of how these images are used are presented as follows:

"Sun"

"Sun" is a poignant image in Enekwe's poetry and suggests brilliance, strength and valour. These all have positive connotations. We encounter the sun along with active verbs suggestive of positive action. The centrifugal brilliance of the sun can be contrasted with the passive receptivity of the moon: "When the sun will darken/ and grow cold?" (*Kilimanjaro* 34); "the sun smiles in the day/ sun's cream on frozen streams" (9); "Sunset glitters in/ a basket of gold" (16); "One day, a brush of sunrays/ shall sweep away/ all this" (19); "sons of the sun" (44); "Neto crawled through the womb of isolation/ into the firm sunshine of war" (53).

"Rain"

When "Rain" recurs in Enekwe's poetry the idea of life, sustenance, revival, regeneration and health abounds. Of course these are all positive associations. Sometimes this favourable weather is contrasted with the harsh West African "Harmattan" whose associations are quite in opposition with man. In the examples below, rain functions as an agent of restoration: "Raindrops endow them with their colours/ until they all dissolve in the perpetual/ moulding of the earth" (*Pots* 21); "They are like rain /that falls in Harmattan" (25); "let your rains /falling wash /dust to dust /underfoot…" (8).

"Winter"

The winter of the Occident is revealed through Enekwe's poetry as harsh and debilitating. Its other qualities are stultification, suffocation and death. The image also connotes poor physical and mental condition. For example, the idea of winter in the poem "Joker" shows unfavourable and unhealthy conditions imposed on man by this weather. Man in a bid to survive resorts to measures such as wearing animal feathers – which, by means of semantic extension, "turn them into animals". In the poem, "Mandatory song" (*Kilimanjaro* 13), winter embodies the tragedy of modern youth in their tendency to self annihilation. They suffer terribly (in "burning winter") by their search for "fleeting contentment" (13). Further example is found in "the river yielded itself/ to winter's smothering embrace" (*Kilimanjaro* 18).

"Harmattan"

The West African harmattan denotes the harsh climate of dryness and aridity in the land and, in some instances, evokes death and forcible departure to the unknown: "… friends lost in harmattan haze" (*Kilimanjaro* 12);

> Harmattan is here
> to make things dry
> …
> its dry fingers soften the soil
> for the roots to pass.
> (*Gentle* 25)

"They are like rain /that fall in Harmattan" (*Pots* 25); "When Harmattan has settled /to rule or ruin" (28).

"Wave"

Here the poet focuses on the restless, yet enduring, movements of sea and ocean waves in his poetry. This idea projects tumult and uncertainty in a time of violence and destruction. The connotation is discernible in the following lines:

> I love the wave as friend
> and foe, for its tumult
> washes sand from stone
> shakes the vein to sense; (*Pots* 16)

"Pardon the misery of flowers/ rushed by fetid waters" (*Kilimanjaro* 12); and "We meet in season/ as surf and crag /often as we part" (*Pots* 14).

"Wind"

The wind is equal to the sea and waves in restlessness. Ideas communicated by the activity of the wind may be positive while, in other instances, they are quite undesirable. In all, the world is imbued with life by wind. This awareness finds a fitting parallel in Placide Temple's observation about forces in African ontology:

> The world ... is spirit and that every form of existence is in essence a vital force, a force which is not an *attribute* of the being or thing, but which *is* that being or thing itself. That which enhances the vital force is good; that which diminishes it is bad. A man, a stone, a tiger, a twig each has or, more properly, is a manifestation of a vital force which can be increased or diminished by events. (46)

The ultimate end associated with wind and sea waves is eternity, death, permanence or infinity. We find this instance in the following uses: "Think of all the pieces of cloud /sailing gently to eternity" (*Kilimanjaro* 10); "She rode on the wings of the wind /like a flower rushed in a storm"; "She is gone with the wind of eternity /dark traces dancing in the gloom" (*Pots* 2);

> but dust, coming
> with the wind
> laid thick on it. (8)

"Mud" and "Dust" and 'Stone"

Other recurrent images that always suggest death in Enekwe's poetry are "mud", "stone" and "dust". Mud and dust communicate the knowledge that the physical part is dead. The poet's use of them with their implied associations is consonant with communal African regard for mud and dust as things of death. We also find Christian religious references to creation and death in these objects although there are layers of differences in their traditional and Christian usage.

"Mud"

"Mud" conveys the idea of something encased and in the process of putrefaction. It is wet and heavy with all the organs of decay working vigorously to disintegrate and break them up. By extension, it denotes different phases of societal degeneration: "abandoned mud forms of their mates" (*Pots* 27); "voices of humanity trapped in mud" (*Kilimajaro*11). This impression extends to other poems: "…we made gods of them out of mud and copper (*Pots* 10); "the mud dam bursts" (7); "where the worms that groan endlessly in the/mud" (21); "mud-smudged twigs on mounds" (20).

"Dust"

By the recurrence of "dust" the poet forcefully projects the abject and irretrievable deadness of an object mixed with sand to become indistinguishable from the soil. Compared with the previous allusion, we can say that while mud is the piece of earth that has individual identity, dust refers to earth mounds no longer distinguishable from the soil. By extension dust and mud instil an awareness of a time span or, in the case of "Story of Ceylonese Girl", the death which makes the human corpse indistinguishable from the soil. This idea of what we might call "instant death and mixture with the earth", is a negation of spiritual order and recurs in most of Enekwe's war poems like in the lines: "soldiers marched, kissed the dust" (*Pots* 10); "his body drawn in the dust that could not rise enough/ to tell his people of his whereabouts" (21); "faraway from the dust of her own dear land" (2); "Falling wash/ dust to dust" (8); "and dark dust scrape/ with bangle-topped sandals"; "lie among the dust and bones of earth" (25);

> but dust, coming
> with the wind
> laid thick on it. (8)

"Stone"

The stone cuts an image of lifelessness with its associated cold dryness. This image collocates with death. As in his use of "harmattan", "white" and "winter", the poet resorts to this image when he seeks a euphemism for death – or for something about to die. In "Mass for the Dead", the poet refers to the soldiers aimlessly marching "under stone-heavy kits" (*Pots* 27), which implies their imminent death. Enekwe's portraiture of endemic death, with its mood of despair and hopelessness, is seen in the following instances: "what purpose surge stray roots/ among cold-faced stones"; "…sharpen/ on the crooked stone/ the dull edges of our hearts" (4); "…stop a falling rock" (2); "They are dry pebbles waiting on the beach" (6).

III) COLOURS

There are recurrent references to colours Enekwe's poetry. In many poems these colours help communicate a sense of irony and contrasts. Some colours repeatedly suggest something positive and desirable while others are not of salutary effect.

Positive colours

The colours "green" and "gold" recur as beautiful, warm and positive associations as shown below:

"Gold"

Used more in the collection *Marching to Kilimanjaro*, the colour of gold has the positive association of royalty, success and wealth as seen in the following: "Dante walks across the gold bridge" (*Kilimanjaro* 13), "sunset glitters in a basket of gold" (16); "There is gold-dust in your blood" (*Pots* 36).

"Green"

"Green" is used to connote fertility, freshness and by extension life: "Let life sprout, green /at the urging of rains" (*Kilimanjaro* 37); "Green grass, trim, velvet" (55); "… hills are covered /with deep green grass" (*Gentle* 37).

Negative colours

"Blue" and "Yellow"

"Blue" and "yellow" are suggestive of unnatural glamour as evidenced in the following lines: "where blue lights flicker" (*Kilimanjaro* 31); "Yellow feelings where injustice reigns/ yellow life of the poor/ yellow light at dusk when drunken books shrivel" (25) and "roads, like yellow ribbons stretch to the/ end of the world" (*Gentle* 37).

"White"

The colour white is a purview of disease, of something leprous, ghostly or deadly, as in the examples of men who "shoot white clouds through their nostrils" (*Pots* 1);

> when hate burns us white

    from coal black to dazzle ash
    -the only way to be white. (18)

In addition, "The flames are white/ morning or sunset" (26). On occasion, though, white is made to refer to cleanness and purity when it functions in synonym with the ethereal: "Her teeth were white as the morning sky" (38).

"Purple"

The purple colour is the harbinger of bloodbath and death. It is portentous of imminent violent destruction as in the examples: "Slowly your life spread /purple about you"; "to keep your soul/ from escaping in the purple flow" (*Pots* 23); "purple newsblast" (*Kilimanjaro* 12); "dusk and purple light over lovely/ Salisbury" (55);

    hair will grow again
    on the mouldy scars of time
    of the purple battleground. (63)

IV) NAMES: HEROES AND VILLAINS

Like the traditional artiste is accustomed to doing, Enekwe has a reel of names of actual people in his poems. This serves as a means of associating favourable or opposite qualities to the people mentioned. Hence a name may signify the positive or negative tendencies associated with such an individual or society. In his poetry there is a repertoire of actual names that represent contrasting qualities of a hero or a villain as shown below.

Heroes:

Nzeogwu, Achibong, Atuegwu, Okigbo, Pol Ndu, Dr Alvan Ikoku, Chinua Achebe, Emma Obiechina, Mathis Kulersegaram, Pablo Neruda, Joe and Carol Bruchac and family, Gen Mamman

Vatsa, Nnabuenyi Ugonna, Agbogho Mmonwu, Samora Machel, Oliver Tambo, Antonio Agostingho Neto, Mugabe, Mandela, Nyerere, (Murtala) Mohammed, Ekumeku, Steve Biko and Martin Utsu, among others, form the pantheon of heroes of Enekwe's Afrocentric vision.

Villains:

The range of world villains in the poems may include names like Cantigny and Iwojima, Napoleon, Patton, Cindy, Mandatory, the Belgium (colonial) Masters, (French) Legionaires, Walls (of Apartheid, Berlin, etc.), Vorster, (the entire) French Legion, (political) Dictators and Helen (of the Trojan war).

V) BODY

The poet hardly refers to man as a complete being, thus emphasising the fragmentation that abounds in society. All through Enekwe's oeuvres, references are often made to body parts of a human being in a transient sense, and with clinical detachment. For instance, images of death are represented as "skull" and "bones": "seared monograms of skull and bones" (*Pots* 27); "lie among the dust and bones of earth" (25); "the lone thought/ in her cold skull" (5); "Skull and bones of a Biafra lover" (2). Human frailty and lack of restraint are described as the "pelvis" that "gyrates in a flame dance" (*Kilimanjaro* 1) or "drops of man /between breasts" (6) or "stench/ of rotten tongues between molars" (9);

> Their arrogance is firm
> as the prick of a babe
> about to wet its crib. (*Kilimanjaro* 28);
>
> Your warm breasts
> light in the corridors of life

your lips, two petals pressed together. (29)

More indices of sexual voyeurism in body talks abound in the lines: "your lifted thigh/deflects the planets" (31); "tender bowels / laden with slime" (30); "tickle the nipples/ of tipsy ladies"; "spray your anus /with eau de cologne"(33); "hunger dynamites the brain" (37); "hunger gnaws his belly/ wintry winds nip his chest"(38); "tongues of acid/burning faces/ searing eyes" (40).

VI) FAUNA AND FLORA
Birds

Enekwe's poetry recognises two types of birds: the normal birds and predator birds, hence the usual paradoxes of the admirable and dreadful. As an image of innocence, the poet would refer to a bird, or birds, to convey the quality of virtue, of being alive and being lively, natural and able to soar above physical limitations:

> A bird rides the waves
> and does not know
> the secrets of the sea
>
> Chukwu's silent arms
> are unknown
> by the birds
> they buoy along. (*Pots* 15)

In "Too Long in the city" the poet laments: "No bough from which my birds/ can rebound from ordinariness" (*Kilimanjaro* 17); "Death by bullets is no death at all/ ask the Phoenix for confirmation" (*Pots* 9). "The birds have since/ fled her walls/ the last leaves/ on their beaks" (5).

A striking parallel to this image comes in the motif of flight. Enekwe resonates the dream of soaring upward and away into the skies, and into eternity. For the poet, the flight of birds, particularly, is a release, the ultimate movement that leads to human progress. It can also lead to attainment of spiritual epiphany, thus abandoning the mundane on the hard, stony and muddy earth. We are witnesses to this perceptivity in the poem "Mmonwu": "dancing jewel/ teach me to fly..."; "fleet/ wriggle/ and make miracle figures in space" (*Kilimanjaro* 2).

Predator "Hawk"

However, for Enekwe, not all the birds of nature are admirable. One, particularly the hawk, is a predator that feeds off smaller birds. In "A Land of Freedom" a hero's betrayal is seemingly justified by the ill will of his enemies: "they called him a hawk/ and murdered him" (3). This position of the people that their "Osagyefo" had turned a "killer-bird" contrasts sharply with their earlier praise for him as a saviour who "found for them/ a new farm in the east" (3). Here is a case of mob vacillation that points to the poet's contempt for the crowd, a subtle note in Enekwe's and few other Nigerian verses. The poet, in his irony, identifies the "crowd" as the real "hawk" that undid its hapless benefactor without just cause. Another example of the predator bird is found in the lines, "out of the clear sky/ a hawk swoops at the frail beauty"(*Pots* 32).

Sometimes the poet uses the bird image for farce, as in the irony on how man is turned into an animal as a result of the weather (winter) which forces him to dress up in coats made of animal skins and feathers: "coats fat/ with hair or feathers"; "and all that make men/ walking birds"(1).

"Worms"

Worms and maggots are metaphors for the maintenance of cyclic balance in the regenerative activity of nature. The poet perceives this act as a natural phenomenon that serves its purpose in the ecological structure: "maggots have chewed and moulded/ these frames and hues back to earth". Thus in few instances where references are made to "worms", they are to expatiate the idea of maintaining a natural rhythm: "for from dust to dust the drum rolls" (*Pots* 6);

> Worms blow you
> through their warm bellies
> back into the womb
>
> far deep in the turning crusts
> far far with the rhythm of rains. (9)

These lines communicate a sense of the cyclic order of life and nature: "where the worms that groan endlessly in the mud/ tumble them through their guts/ making a clamour within the crusts of eternity" (21); "Shoots below caress the worms that in search of melody/ blow in vain the flutes of our bones" (20).

"Lion"

This animal appears in Enekwe's poems especially in the collection *Marching to Kilimanjaro*. The association of lion as "king of the animals" (*Pots* 13) is drawn from folklore. We can note this idea in the following lines: "home of lion, lioness/ and their golden haired cubs" (*Kilimanjaro* 22); "Suddenly like a lion/ you tear the wind" (57); "In our hearts, African Lions rage" (59);

> Gently the lion wakes
> ...he plants his legs
> upon a path. (45)

"Trees", "Leaves" and "Grass"

Recurrent in Enekwe's poetry is the image of "trees", "leaves" and "grass". Trees in African ontology symbolise strength, stoicism, firmness and growth of the race. Among the trees of many an Igbo proverb or idiom, the "Iroko" comes out most kingly. It is repeatedly used in Enekwe's poems as in Achebe's novels. It is this Iroko tree which grows in the rain forests of Africa, notable for its huge trunks, towering heights and great foliage, that endows strength, power, protection, nobility, firmness and many other great qualities that accompany its dignified presence: mother "... planted/ a love that thrives like Iroko" (12). Thus the image of this tree beheaded is a signpost to great tragedy:

> so like the beheaded Iroko
> you stood till blasted
> to the roots. (*Pots* 22)

Of further significance are the leaves that grow on trees and grass on the soil. In a poem to the memory of Alvan Ikoku, Enekwe testifies that "Great men are not plucked from trees /they are the lone leaf sailing /the glitter, on the sea" (25). The image of "a land growing grassless from a scorching air" is poignant with the picture of desertification and environmental degradation. Further in "The Story of a Ceylonese Girl" there is the grassless aridity of an environment despoiled by war. In contrast "the air of flowers and motherhood" (9) shows life and vitality. The child is "a mere sapling" (11); some crying voices are "husky ... as people who eat too much corn" (13), and Neruda

> ... sang of love
> that nourishes the tiniest leaves
> on the oak. (9)

Here "leaves" and "oak" are used as icons of life as against the implied physical death of the valiant one. And to show how deeply our so-called civilisation has made us never the same people anymore, there is the image of "an Iroko deep-rooted and shod/ among an ancient wood" (*Kilimanjaro* 23).

VII) PROVERBS

There are few proverbs in Enekwe's poetry and this might not necessarily mean the poet's lack of confidence on this prose device for his poetry. Use of African proverbs comes out better in the longer narrative forms where such a lack may point to a "general diminution of African values"(77) as the duo of Cope and Chester have claimed. However, here are some of the few that Enekwe uses. Incidentally the proverbs have retained their traditional meaning and cultural association: "dogs bite the fingers /that gave them bones" (*Pots* 25), in reference to human ingratitude; "and pursue mice while flames dance on the crowns of your huts" (19) as an allusion to the misplaced priorities of modern Nigerian society. "His mother.../waits as double night threatens her son" (28), in reference to certain tragedy and death. "Life, they say, is war that ends in death" (32) meaning the futility of all earthly or worldly pursuits; "Where the hawk and the eagle can perch /none displacing the other" (*Kilimanjaro* 26) deferring to the need for equal rights and justice in human affairs.

VIII) BIBLICAL REFERENCES

As with proverbs, Enekwe does not use many Biblical references in his poems. Few Afrocentric scholars would adopt a wholesale orthodox teleological construct in any case. However there are some references to Armageddon and Original sin doctrines of the Bible: "on that day, the rivers, even the mighty ones/ will turn to stone, and trees will rush like warriors" (*Pots* 19); and "the sin of my people/ upon my people" (19).

IX) FOLKLORE

Enekwe has made few use of folkloric image and ideas drawn from African folk tales, myths and legends. In all three collections of poems we have just the following: (a) "to chant beyond the seven hills/ where eagles weave crowns/ for the subjects of our song" (*Pots* 25); (b) "Across seven seas I flew/ a bird of passage with a passing song" (*Kilimanjaro* 22); (c) "Across the seven hills/ where smoke and vapour boil" (*Pots* 35). The motif of "seven hills" appears in tales to denote the crossing into ancestral realms, also called "land of the dead". Here it signifies the long distance one must traverse in order to achieve greatness.

Laying preponderance on the difficulty of the enterprise, "crossing seven hills, rivers", further suggests an attempt of supernatural significance – something very far away or hardly attainable by mundane humanity. Hence it is not surprising, for instance, that unity proved a hollow slogan in Nigeria with the pogrom and war that ensued (see the poem "Unity"in *Broken Pots*). With reference to (a) above, the poet seeks to lay emphasis on the difficulty entailed for one seeking to be a hero, while (b) foreshadows the difficulties surmounted by the poet before his temporary exile for studies abroad. Another subtle use of oratorical features is seen in the lines of the song:

> Heaven and earth listen to our cry
> Songs of wind and leaves ...
> mud-smudged twigs on mounds. (*Pots* 20)

"Heaven and earth listen to our cry" is drawn from the song popular in the Biafran enclave during the war. It was a supplication to the ancestral guardians of a bewildered nation, affirming the collective survival spirit of the doomed. Thus "Ripples of the Apocalypse" is made to communicate the despair, misery and despondency of a race

visited with genocide and complicity by other ethnic nationalities of the federation during the debacle of the late sixties.

CONCLUSION

What may be gleaned from this study is that Enekwe's poetry is purposely rich with images drawn from the flora and fauna of his environment. They are plumbed between positive and negative connotations as a technique to sustain the ironies and twists of a largely diagolic conversation. While some of these images conform to their general associations, some are re-inscribed in new ideas and meanings within the poetic discourse. In other instances, some associations are "stock" in the sense that their semantic interpretation remains constant whenever and wherever they occur. For instance, the idea associated with the colour "yellow" as something "sickly' and "unnatural" is so constant even when it occurs among positive symbols as in the poem "That I could Fly":

> hamlets blossom in the midst of trees
> and roads, like yellow ribbons
> stretch to the end of the world. (*Gentle* 37)

In *Gentle Birds* collection, if "yellow" and "ribbons" should represent the allure of civilisation in an otherwise natural or stable world, then the poet's attempt not to bury meaning in images (because he uses so few in this children's poetry), and his perception of Western civilisation as defiled by its exploitation and imperialism, still resonate by implication of the colour yellow. Also in "The voice of waters", the persona consorts with an "old lady" with "teeth... white as the morning /sky" (*Pots* 38, *Gentle* 41) – an affirmative image but possibly also depreciative from other observations of Enekwe's use of "white" as a blighting experience.

Thus despite the poet's attempt at presenting an old woman with energy and vigour, we know that her "white teeth" and "the vigour of the river" associate with the river's "end of its journey", and birds "gliding forever", to forecast imminent demise. By this hindsight, we are pushed to seek potential ambivalence of meaning. We can equally deduce that water, like the old woman, has both the capacity of nurturing life (which is what the poet attempts to show in the poem) and also death as envisioned in the waves that "deposit" the "sweat and salt /of humanity" (42).

In *Gentle Birds* the poet's pre-occupation with nature images reads as a summation of a ritual quest for identity symbolised in the great birds of Africa's fauna. We are nudged to perceive the poet's pre-occupation with the elements: sun, rain, birds and water, and his ideas about African freedom and unity ("Mandela"), from a conglomerate of images where the bird towers above all. Enekwe's admiration for these winged creatures is articulated through his constant projection of them as "teachers", "friends", "instructors", "inspirers", etc. In fact, "birds" appear to be for the poet what "nature" is for Wordsworth.

There is a further comparative note on the part of the poet with birds and men. Perhaps this distinguishes his references to nature from that of English Romantic poets. From the reference to birds we can gain an insight to the motif of flight and motion which pre-occupies the poet's imagination in many instances. This motif, seen as flight in the case of birds, is also strongly communicated through the movement of waves and wind as harbingers, nay conveyors, of man's journey into eternity.

Flight for the poet is a means of overcoming, conquering or surmounting difficulties, problems and obstacles; it is the means of freeing "the flesh/ from the muffle of dust" (*Kilimanjaro* 2). This appears to be the vision of Enekwe's poetry: that the vessel of man, like the different "pots" muted in his verse, must definitely "break" (die): the "pot of water/ has slipped and crumbled/ while its little fountain/lingers into our farm". But then what follows? Do we cry "like the wail of a lost lamb", or mourn like "husky ones ...who eat too much corn" and "make too much love"? Or do we "... strike our drums/ and tune our chords/... till we burst our drums/... and marvel at the strain/ in the carving of heroes" (*Pots* 25)?

There is no doubt the poet expects us to embrace the latter as an ennobling reaffirmation of existence. In Enekwe's poetry, Keatian fatalism, in the annihilation of self as an inevitable "home-call", is apparently farcical. This idea is informed by an African world construct that "affirms the trinity of the dead, the living and the yet unborn as the eternal cyclic order in which the rites of passage of the living form only an infinitesimal journey or stage" (Emezue 4). Hence death loses its bite because, as the poet severally observes, the dead is only "a seed/ at the moment of germination" (*Kilimanjaro* 46) and "mere victims of the world" (*Pots* 25). For the poet, there "is no fence/ no dead or living; the dead are distant friends /who refuse to write or call" (29).

WORKS CITED

Abrams, M. H. *Glossary of Literary Terms*. Orlando: Harcourt Brace Jovanovich, 1993.

Cope, J. S. & K. A. Chester. "'Stealing the White Man's Weapon or Forging One's Own?' African and African-American English in Ce's *Children of Koloko* and Morrison's *Beloved*." *The Works of Chin Ce. Critical Supplement (A) 1:* Ed. Irene Marques. IRCALC, 2007. 63-85.

Diop, Chiek Anta. *The Cultural Unity of Black Africa: The Domains of*

Patriarchy and of Matriarchy in Classical Antiquity. London: Karnak House, 1989.

Dudley, Sharia. "Theory in Praxis: Matrifocal Feminism and *The Lianja Epic*." *The African Journal of New Poetry. NP.4*. IRCALC, 2007. 37-58.

Emezue, G. M. T. *Comparative Studies in African Dirge Poetry*. Enugu: Handel Books, 2001.

Enekwe, O. O. *Broken Pots*. New York: Greenfield Review Press, 1977.

———. *Marching to Kilimanjaro*. Nsukka: Afa Press, 2005.

———. *Gentle Birds come to me*. Nsukka: Afa Press, 2007.

———. "Interview with Zulu Sofola." *Okike: An African Journal of New Writing*. No. 27/28, 1988. 56-66.

Placide Tempels. *La Philosophic Bantoue* Paris: Edition Africaines, 1949.

Sofola, Zulu. *The Artist and the Tragedy of a Nation*. Ibadan: Caltop Publications, 1994.

Spurgeon, Caroline. *Shakespeare's Imagery*. London: Cambridge University Press, 1968.

3

"Broken Pots"
THE LANGUAGE OF ENEKWE'S POETRY
C. L. Ngonebu

> The rise of cultural nationalism in the 1960s has as its major consequence the need to valorize African culture as a way of deconstructing the modernist episteme of the invading Occident.
> -*Pius Adesanmi, "Ville Cruelle?"*

> Of course, unanimity exists at the most general level of statement, that literature is a way of doing things with words....
> -*A. N. Akwanya "... Soyinka's Fiction"*

THESE statements by Pius Adesanmi (44) and A. N. Akwanya (55) lead us to a close examination of the syntactic aberrations that culminate in making "Broken Pots" a representation of the archetypical conflict between traditional and modern values – a conflict which has been at the crux of many African writings be it poetry, drama, or prose, even up to the present. Thus the focus of this paper on the device of syntactic aberrations evident in the poem "Broken Pots" is aimed at examining how the poet uses such linguistic device to project a vision of a world devastated by forces beyond the control of the African land. Since a writer has the freedom to use language in various ways to achieve his/her aim, Enekwe employs this linguistic technique for the purpose of creating a work of artistic beauty and social relevance.

Every literary artist has a purpose of writing, a reality which he/she wants to put across to the reader. This is why literature is one of the greatest tools for shaping, exploring, and defining the human society. As Nnolim puts it, "it is part and parcel of our everyday lives no matter how savage, primitive, or technologically advanced our society is" (88-9). The challenge posed by literature in human society is great. Literature exposes social ills and problems and proffers solutions to them; it examines issues and concretizes them; it delves into unknown realms and makes prophetic statements; it establishes myths and perpetuates them; it instigates mass consciousness and social transformation; it raises our hopes and can dash those. Whichever direction the artist takes, however, literature makes one form of statement or another.

In making these statements and in exploring varied themes, the primary instrument of the literary artist is language. Apart from being the most important tool available to humanity, language is the medium of literary creation. Again in the words of Nnolim:

> Just as in the fine arts where the artist uses colour, lines, curves, light and shade plus perspective to produce an object of beauty, literature achieves the same effects through the use of words .... So, in literature, words are used to produce peculiar effects that entertain us, that give us enjoyment. (86-87)

Poetry is one form of literature that derives much impetus from the creative and imaginative embellishments of language. According to Nwoga, poetry is an enjoyable medium through which deep thoughts and feelings are expressed, through which significant experiences and perceptions are conveyed, *in language modified for beauty* [emphasis mine] (193). In creating poetry, the poet has the freedom to stretch his/her hand beyond the confines of the language code and make use of varied linguistic techniques: syntactic, semantic and phonological patterning. Justifying poetic freedom, Nwoga further notes:

> The devices used by the poets are available in ordinary communication, but in poetry, these devices are concentrated – varieties of rhythm, manipulation of sound effects, vividness through concrete images taken from the environment, wit and other forms of mental adaptation....(193)

The Nigerian scholar then concludes by saying that "not all poems use all the devices but the good poet uses those which are adequate for his theme and the image and experience he wishes to express and communicate" (193). This is not surprising because a poet has the freedom to use language in "unfamiliar and potentially confusing ways" (qtd. in Akwanya, 49), and to range over wide expanse of linguistic conventions in order to portray a particular theme. Geoffrey Leech says that "man needs to express himself superabundantly on matters which affect him deeply" (84). Egonu shares this view when he opines that the writer makes a conscious and deliberate choice and arrangement of both words and imagery in order to produce certain effects on the reader, not only by what is said but also by how it is said (143). F. S. Scott is quoted by Chapman to have fostered the idea that "the writer's style is often expressed as much by the grammatical clauses and structures he prefers as by his choice of words" (44).

When we examine the style of syntactic aberrations evident in the poem "Broken Pots", we will, in the process, unravel the "unfamiliar" and "potentially confusing ways" in which language is employed for its connotative rather than denotative; symbolic rather than literal; figurative rather than plain (Nnolim 89) meaning. This misleading language of literature, as Akwanya asserts, calls for commentary and interpretation by the critic whose role it is to bring the text to life. He is the one through whom the passive text breaks its silence, while remaining silent, the machine that is the 'life' of the text-as-a-perlocutionary act (49).

Of all other linguistic patterns in the poem, it is the syntactic structures that bring the message of the poem to the forecourt of the reader's mind, for, in the words of T. S. Eliot, "only by the form, the pattern, can words and music reach the stillness" (Norton II: 140-412). A similar analysis on the syntactic deviations in "Broken Pots" was done by Anohu who examined the syntactic and lexical structures that act as elements of coherence and cohesion in the poem. This chapter, however hopes to take the analysis of "Broken Pots" further by expostulating the deeper meanings that emerge from the language of Enekwe's poem.

The poem "Broken Pots" is made up of five long complex sentences, which we can also call stanza. Each long sentence or stanza is marked off by a full stop. Each line runs into the other. What this shows is that the experience the poet is exploring is a complex one, serious and painful. The loss of virtue and of glory is not something to be dismissed in a brief discourse. A rape or a desecration is a mighty crime.

The poem can be roughly divided into two parts, which Agu posits gives it a certain sense of movement and stillness, a structural duality... which helps to evoke the sober feeling of tragedy... (103). The first part portrays the rich, lovely, serene, unsoiled world of Africa, while the remaining part is a lamentation at the loss of that which was once adorable. Both parts are unified by the syntactic deviations in the poem for, as Anohu asserts, this is a unifying linguistic strategy which Enekwe has successfully used in merging theme and form effectively (47). The first part can be compared to the romantic poetry of adoration of beauty and nature. This sub-theme is presented in profuse syntax: In this pattern, we have the same structure of

Det + Adj + Adj + N:

The | Heavy | bosomed | hill
    | Winding | narrow | path

Although they are syntagmatically related as they share the same features, both structures actually contrast each other. One is an adjective of maturity, ripeness, heaviness and succulence. The other, like the seven lean corns of Pharaoh's dream in the Bible, shows thinness, fragility, and stunted growth, hence their antonymous relationship. However, by occurring in the same parallel structure they have been imbued with the same value. In Africa the gigantic and the rich lie close to and combine with the plain and the simple to form its whole scenery. It is this same parallel that Gladys Casely-Hayford draws in her poem "Freetown" where she says that when God made Freetown, He scattered small bays and small inlets close to mighty hills to watch over the tranquil city.

Taking the phrase "bosomed hill", we have a case of selectional rule violation. "Bosomed" in usage is a feature of full-fledged womanhood. But the poet has attributed this female quality to an inanimate thing the hill. In using this attribute, the poet wants to attract our attention to the hill. He wishes to emphasize that the hill is not only huge but also attractive and imposing, like the figure of a shapely woman. He wants us to see the beauty in traditional Africa by comparing it to that of a woman in her prime. The two noun phrases "hill" and "path" feature with equal dignity. They enhance the richness of the continent. Within the same stanza we have the parallel structures:

Lies …		hut
	our	
Stumbles...		farm

"Lies" and "stumbles" belong to the verbal group and are syntagmatically related to the two noun phrases treated above – "hill" and "path". The two verb phrases show the unconscious intertwining or mingling of picturesque topographic features. However, in the use of the term "stumbles" with the noun phrase "path" we have another violation of selectional restriction rule. While animate beings would stumble and fall, Enekwe, by using this configuration for the "path", is giving us a hint of what will happen later in the poem and by extension in Africa: Unintentionally, Africans will kill the goose that lays the golden egg; that is, they will cause the destruction of values that had led them through all these ages.

"Hut" and "farm" are other features of the rustic life, which are characteristics of traditional Africa. This glorification continues with the presentation of animals that are gay and carefree, as if they too knew and felt the beauty in nature:

| The | squirrels | prance |
| | … birds | twitter |

The two noun phrases "squirrels" and "birds" are synonymously related. They are a microcosm of the entire animal kingdom for which Africa is known and admired. Their prancing and twittering are signs of happiness in this world of peace and tranquility. This part of the poem has a romantic touch. It takes our minds back to the poetry of the romanticists whose pre-occupation was the exploration of the unadulterated simple rural countryside.

Then comes the second part of the poem – the breaking of the pot

– embodied in the lines:

> We always hear, soft and clear,
> Like the wail of lost lamb,
> The voice of a virgin
> Whose pot of water
> Has slipped and crumbled. (15-19)

This part about the breaking of the pot is a signifier, which lends itself to various interpretations /significations. The two verb phrases used to show this break – "slipped" and "crumbled" – share the semantic feature of "destruction, breakage, irreparable loss". Enekwe is, in the words of Widdowson, "struggling to devise patterns of language which will bestow upon the linguistic items concerned just those values which will convey his personal vision" (42). For Anohu, "slipped" and "crumbled" are so functionally cohesive in their patterning since they collectively suggest a situation that would cue in losses or damages. At least, she continues, "a precarious atmosphere is so effectively created that when we eventually learn of the things that are broken, lost, or disintegrated (either at a personal level or at a collective level), we are hardly surprised" (46). Hence, what the poet implies here, by the use of these syntactic structures, is that the destruction of rich African values was inadvertently done by people oblivious of the dire consequences.

At one level, making allusion to "the voice of a virgin", breaking of the pot symbolizes a rape, or loss of virginity. It is only the loss of something valuable that can elicit "a wail" like that "of a lost lamb" or one, which, because the poet is too young, he cannot name (Ln 22-23). Further at a broader level, the pot is a metaphor of wholeness, of serenity and tranquility. By extension, the breaking of the pot signifies the destruction of the virtues of rustic rural life. Its breaking denotes the chaos and anomie that result from a society torn apart from its values, a society unable to sustain its populace. This breaking symbolizes the fragmentation that Africa suffered, a fragmentation which, according to Oladipo, has caused us to lose sight of our origins, made us exiles from our authentic values and traditions (72), thereby ensuring that our journey on the path of development "has been a going against our self, a journey into our killer's desire" (Armah 2). That is why the twittering and happiness in the poem suddenly comes to an end. We then hear "soft and clear"

                        | wail...
         The | voice..
                        | cry..

of the people. It is true that something serious has happened and the poet uses these three equivalent terms to underline the lamentation and the sorrow of the people who have lost their identity. The poet goes further to classify the voices he heard as a means of intensifying the emotions of the deprived people:

                        | husky | ones
         And | muted | (voices)
                        | (others)

"Husky, muted, (others)" have the same syntactic structure, as they are all adjectives describing the cries of the people. The poet could as well have used only one word, "voice", to describe the phenomena. But he wants to personify vividly and explicitly the pain, the heartache, as conveyed by the nature of their voices. This is the cry of a people oppressed, exploited and deprived of basic social living condition, bedeviled by myriads of problems: cultural dislocation, perversion of values, misuse of skills, lack of unity, incompetent and derelict leaders, chaotic governance, under-development, and poverty.

The breaking of the pot is a symbolic representation of the loss of a gem, the decimation of those values that sustained the people in the past. The poet's inability to grasp and "name" the totality of the voices of the people in agony arises from the deep confusion which the decimation of the people's culture has thrown them into. This is what Obiechina brings out when he states:

> Social change in West Africa is proceeding at a rapid rate. Old values are quickly crumbling and solid new ones are evolving as rapidly with the result that there is confusion in the minds of many. (qtd. in Akwanya 47)

Just as the people of Africa lost their virtue, glory, or identity, so too is their smooth soft voice, which becomes "husky" and "mute", changed by their bitter experience, and hardened by their sorrow.

It is worthy to mention that Anohu sees "Broken Pots" differently. According to her, it is the necessary and sometimes unconscious process of the regeneration of a sphinx (47). Perhaps, we can accept this interpretation if we appreciate the fact that a seed has to die for it to germinate and grow into a tree that yields multitudes of fruits.

In the same vein, we can assert that Africa has to go through the tough and difficult times before it emerges as a continent to be reckoned with in the world. "Broken Pots" is a poem that exhibits layers of meaning. What we have, therefore, tried to establish in this chapter is that the poet has been able to express varied painful realities by the subtle manipulation of syntax, and expert configuration of thought and language.

Works Cited

Adesanmi, P. "Ville Curelle? Literature's Tragic Paradox." *Okike: An African Journel of New Writing.* 37, 1997. 41-49.

Agu, O. "Structure, Theme and Meaning in Onuora Ossie Enekwe's *Broken Pots.*" *Okike: An African Journal of New Writing.* 48, 2006, 102-116.

Akwanya, A. N. "Characterization in Soyinka's Fiction: A Study in Typology." *Okike: An African Journal of New Writing.* 36, 1997. 5-55.

---. "Orthodoxy in African literary Criticism: Need for a New Beginning." *Okike: An African Journal of New Writing* 45, 2000. 44-56.

Anohu, V. "Syntactic Deviation: An Inquiry into the Language of Ossie Enekwe's "Broken Pots." *Okike: An African Journal of New Writing.* 31, 1995. 44-47.

Armah, A. K. *Two Thousand Seasons.* Ibadan: Heinemann Books, 1979.

Casely-Hayford, G. "Freetown." *West African Verse.* London: Longman, 1967.

Chapman, Raymond. *Linguistics and Literature.* London: Edward Arnold, 1975.

Egonu, I. T. K. "Literature and Moral Values. The Role of the African Writer." *Readings in African Humanities: African Perspectives In World Culture.* Ed. I. T. K. Egonu. Owerri: Vivians and Vivians, 1988.

Eliot, T. S. *Burnt Norton.* U. K.: Longman, 1957.

Enekwe, O. *Broken Pots.* Enugu: Government Printer, 1977.

Leech, Geoffrey. *A Linguistic Guide to English Poetry.* London: Longman, 1969.

Nnolim, C. "Writing as Art." *Okike: An African Journal of New Writing.* 49, 2008. 84-93.

Nwoga, D. I. "Utility and Beauty in the African Imagination: The Example of Poetry." *Readings in African Humanities: Traditional and Modern Culture*. Ed. Edith Ihekweazu. Enugu: Fourth Dimension Publishers, 1985. 188-204.

Oladipo, Olusegun. "Historical Retrieval in Ayi Kwei Armah's *Two Thousand Seasons*." *Okike: An African Journal of New Writing*. 41, 1999. 71-82.

Widdowson, H. G. *Stylistics and the Teaching of Literature*. London: Longman, 1975.

4

Poetry and History
ENEKWE ON WAR AND DECADENCE
Sule Egya

OSSIE Onuora Enekwe's poetry, like most of the poetry of his contemporaries, is a product of the time, place and circumstances of its composition. His poems, besides its range of literary devices, have a definitive claim to everyday socio-political issues. The poet's constant burden is to historicise issues through processes of interrogations, inquests, declamations and reclamations. Therefore behind the poetic text is a historical text, the latter as important as the former, designating the nationalist imagination of the poet behind the texts. The poet has thus found a space in what we know as a literature of social commitment whose springboard is what we may call the orthodox African orature where the poet abandons the *self* and assumes the shape of the *other*, his voice that of a town crier, his vision that of a community.

Such poetry, as Nourbese Philip observes, is "rooted in place" (170); it is organically connected to a land by way of identifying with and shepherding the downtrodden of the land towards a positive social vision. In *Broken Pots* and *Marching to Kilimanjaro*, Enekwe is gathering the pieces broken by politicians and tribalists, as tasking as the job is, in order to create a vision for the common people which is as tall as the Kilimanjaro where only the strong may be able to access. In doing this, Enekwe, with an engaging paradox as a trope, negotiates a space between the heavily burdened past and the inevitably hazy future. To be able to speak from this position, the poet must have a bold voice and a strong dream. Throughout Enekwe's two volumes mentioned above, he is vociferous, uncompromising and forthright. He exemplifies Gabriel Okara's kind of poet: "[who] must … exercise the powers of the Word to realise his visions" (78). Enekwe's strength as a poet is that he understands how to exercise the powers in the word and how to redirect such powers to the cause of humanity. With this power of the word he historicises the Nigerian civil war (1967-1970) in which he participated fighting on the side of Biafra.

"THE STORY OF A CEYLONESE GIRL"

Unlike Festus Iyayi who, according to Ferdinand Asoo, "examines the war in the context of its class nature," (250), Enekwe approaches the subject of the war through the human angle. This angle translates to an ideological position, which literature, if we accept Terry Eagleton's conclusion, is said to ultimately be (22). It is not the mainstream position of politicians and thoughtless citizenry; it is not the position that is meant to please those who managed the war at governmental level; nor is it the position of bigots and tribalists seeking sympathy with lame logic. It is the position of a humanist genuinely forging a counter-narrative in the welter of self-righteous narratives that have been trailing the Nigerian civil war. That is why the poet's primary concern is that of the unsung heroes.

Mathi is one of them. Besides projecting the unsung heroine, Enekwe, in "The story of a Ceylonese girl", draws our attention to an interesting side of the war. Beneath the presentation of a foreigner as a fighter for Biafra is an affirmation that the war is an undue brutalisation of a people set to liberate themselves from unbalanced nationhood. The poet uses the story of Mathi to establish a human angle for what he thinks is a just war. It must have been out of sympathy for the oppressed Biafrans that Mathi, a foreigner living in Biafra, chooses to join the war on the side of the Biafra. What should be well understood in this idiom of sacrifice is that Mathi is not moved into the war by its rhetoric, but by the realities of injustice and killings that she has seen. Enekwe's choice of words in this poem, his tone of courage and resignation to fate, and the palpable eulogy that runs through the poem reveal the supra-individual martyrdom that characterises the story of Mathi. Indeed, the poem evokes sympathy not just for Mathi but also for the common Biafrans, especially as it is clear that she takes part in the war for her love of the people:

> Blood of Mathi Kulersegaram
> polluted by battle powder
> Skull and bones of a Biafra lover
> left to smoulder and crack in the flames
> of a city whose paths she loved to walk,
> faraway from the people she loved so much. (1-6)

To show the ugly side of the war, the poet presents Mathi's body smashed and destroyed, and to present the good side of humanity, the poet draws attention to the love that has driven Mathi to destruction. This juxtaposition of the evil of the war and the demonstration of love for humanity is the height of Enekwe's paradox in this poem. In emphasising this paradox – which sees love bringing death instead of life – Enekwe dramatises the Christ-like submission of one's life for the sake of other people. The images of crushed flower and grassless land in the second stanza point to Mathi's deliberate sacrifice for the emancipation of people she loves. She knows there are dangers, she sees the dangers, and she dares the dangers. Certainly before she decides to take arms for the land, she knows that it is a land "crushed and drowned in a restless sea" (12). The intense tone of sadness towards the end of the poems is hinged on the poet's understanding that Mathi's input to the war is overshadowed by the overriding gloom in the land. She dies fighting but her aim is not achieved. From a celebration of courage and bravery, the poem moves to the mourning of a soul lost when she ought to live "to part the hopeful caulk" (20). It therefore reads as an accomplished dirge, as Emezue has pointed out, filled with "the feeling of sadness and longing, the melancholy that comes with departure, separation and consequently nostalgia" (116).

"A PALACE OF TOMES", "NO WAY FOR HEROES TO DIE".

A poem that treats a similar loss of important people and things during the war, though cast in an epigrammatic structure, is "A Palace of Tomes". The subject of the poem is a queen, with her king, along with her tomes, destroyed. Although Enekwe, unlike in the previous poem where a narrative structure is developed, does not describe the destruction of the persona, the expression "her cold skull" (6) either means she is dead or the skull has gone useless. The second stanza affirms the loss:

> The birds have since
> fled her walls
> the last leaves
> in their beaks. (7-10)

Here Enekwe's use of birds as a symbol presents a problem: are the birds of good omen or of bad omen? While the poet seems detached from the queen and her king, he seems attached to

Nzeogwu, Achibong and Atuegwu, the subjects of "No Way for Heroes to Die". Enekwe's vital statement in this poem is that the society tends to forget the ordinary people who fight for its survival and this insensitivity on the part of the society sets humanity adrift. He indicts the society, peopled by "hungry historians and starveling professors" (29), who celebrate anti-heroes and ignore the real heroes of our society. In problematising the concept of heroism in a postcolonial nation such as Nigeria, Enekwe draws our attention to the moral, ethical and cultural values that underpin the socio-political realities of nationhood. What is the process of making a hero in an African nation? Who are those considered heroes in Africa? What is the reward that Africa gives her heroes? Indeed, the Nigerian civil war has continued to provide a premise on which the concept of heroism is constantly re-examined by writers and thinkers in Nigeria. During the war, while the rank and file of the army, on both sides, went to the front and achieved certain feats of exploits, the commanding officers and generals, given to all forms hedonism, making money out of the spillage of innocent blood, stayed back in cities and towns, catching their fun, moving farther backward when war approached. It was those commanding officers and generals who declared themselves heroes, who – as in the case of Olusegun Obasanjo – wrote hagiographies to project a heroism based on morally questionable grounds. In his *My Command*, Obasanjo writes of his "qualities and exploits as an army general and field commander" (135) that account for the victory of Nigeria over Biafra. One of the soldiers in Iyayi's *Heroes* foresees this situation of undue self-praise by the officers:

> After this war many generals will write their account in which they will attempt to show that they were the heroes of this war, that it was their grand strategies that won the war. They will tell the world that they single-handedly fought and won the war. The names of

soldiers like Otun, Emmanuel, Ikeshi and Yemi will never be mentioned....(86)

Like Iyayi, Enekwe reconstructs heroism (really, the history of a people), and by doing that attempts to restore the society to its pre-corruption status. His song is thus non-conformist. Instead of singing to the memories of commanding officers and the generals who have a twisted perception of themselves as heroes, he sings "to the memory of those who died to be forgotten" (1). The interest of the poet here, as he takes to re-writing history, is centring his philosophic quest on those nameless ranks and files who, during the war, were not only killed by weapons but were also destroyed by statistics. "In the field, their scattered bones jeer at the azure sky, and sneer at the masked terrors of rainbows" (7-8). To look upon these ranks and files as heroes is a way of shifting the paradigm from self-praise to true heroism. Every war has its heroes. To determine the heroes of a war is a critical aspect of a post-war history that requires courage, sincerity and faith in nationhood. Poets, perhaps, stand the chance of qualifying as writers of this history, as Enekwe has done in this poem and other poems in the *Broken Pots* collection.

"THE DEFIANT ONE"

Enekwe's discourse on war, apart from projecting true heroism, also focuses on the theme of loss – loss of flesh, of soul, of humanism, and of environment. In fact, loss essentialises the central image of Enekwe's poems of war which is the broken pot, forced to the ground, scattered around, its contents lost to human monstrosities. One of the diverse images the poet uses to expand this pertinent idea is that of the "beheaded Iroko" (6) in the poem "The Defiant One", written to the memory of the late poet Christopher Okigbo. The Iroko is a large tree that casts a wide shade, noted for shelter, sturdiness and protection. Human beings rely on Iroko trees for many things in terms of human survival. If an Iroko loses its "head", its top that casts shade for shelter and protection, then something fundamental to human beings is lost. A reading that sees Okigbo as an Iroko begins from the context that Okigbo is a poet, an artist, whose work has cast a shade for other poets in Nigeria. Seen as the most influential poet in Nigeria even several years after his death, Enekwe's likening him to the great Iroko projects and, at the same time, foregrounds a humanism hinged on the affective essence of art and its all-embracing approach to life. The central idea in this poem is that violence has been done to an innocent, humanist tree that seems courageous and determined to live in spite of the weather:

> You lacked the drift
> of the aged smoke
> ubiquitousness in time
> and colour, despite drought
> and wreckage of the shrine. (1-5)

But the tree has been violently damaged. The damage, given the tenor of the running metaphor, is not only done to the tree alone but also to those who find shelter and protection under it. Such is the damage done to humanity through the killing of Okigbo in the war. Most poets who have written to lament the death of Okigbo take this position (Emezue 58-87); they consider "the vision of the hero as a priceless gem and worthy patriot of immense talents" (71). The dirge in Enekwe's poem has bravery in it. It is the combination of courage and loss: the loss of a courageous soul as a result of which an age "let loose [its] wail" (22).

"TO A FRIEND MADE AND LOST IN WAR."

It is from a different philosophical perspective – that of the inevitability of death – that Enekwe presents another subject of loss to us in "To a Friend Made and Lost in War." Enekwe's philosophical statement in this poem at once moves us to tears and to anger. The idea of postponed death, hoping for life at every survival only to die in spite of hoping, is quite touching. However the reader is angry that death keeps coming until it takes away the hope and life of its victim. Enekwe projects this scenario to remind us that in wartime people hope against hope, seek for survival, feel survival only to be killed in spite of their efforts to live. A sense of frustration and resignation is common at such times, as we see in the utterance of the subject of this poem: "'God may get tired of saving me'" (12). In a way, therefore, the man foresees his own death. But Enekwe's thematic thrust is not the prediction of death in wartime. It is the all-inclusive inhumanity of war that stalks people's lives, whether innocent or not, which has become part of human existence. This is probably why Enekwe concentrates on how the subject of the poem dies:

> Two days later,
> Soviet bomber rockets
> burst your belly
> and tore your intestine
> on the white sheet
> of the hospital bed.
> They bore you weeping
> to another place
> and tried to stitch you,
> to keep your soul
> from escaping in the purple flow.
> But you had too many holes.
>
> So you died among strangers. (14-29)

This vivid portrayal of horror is aimed at showing the cruelty that lives with man in wartime, and the inability of man to escape it. The last line, "We could not find you", speaks of total loss. The poem, symbolic of degeneration from peace to war, begins from hope and ends in total loss. It symbolises a nation set adrift, a heinous movement from the good to the bad, as was the case of Nigeria just after its independence.

"THE SWEET THINGS"

Moving with time, and influenced by the daily happenings in the society, Enekwe's poetry is an engraving in a history that mediates between art and social realities in Nigeria. The experience in Nigeria is that after the war, the society never really gets rebuilt. It may have been physically rebuilt, but the spirit of patriotism and a healthy collective psyche is lost, giving way to the moral and ethical decadence of the 1970s to the 1980s, and to the corrupt militarisation of the polity from the 1980s to the 1990s. What we find in Enekwe's *Marching to Kilimanjaro* is a critical inquest into the human and social affairs of what he calls "an asphyxiated age."

In "The Sweet Things", a name of a pop group in the 1960s, reduced to a paradoxical expression by the poet, what we encounter is moral decadence that comes through in certain images deployed by the poet. In depicting immoralities such as the "Pelvis (which) gyrates in a flame dance" (1) and "Broken faggots over which maggots /carouse with unending turbulence" (3-4), Enekwe makes deeper insinuations that contextualise the wanton mismanagement of natural resources of the land. This poem reminds us of the wasted abundance of an African postcolonial state not just surviving a war but also rediscovering itself in the context of inter-cultural tension. The poem dramatises (and by so doing laments) the shift from the roots, as it were, towards self-alienation and a culture of violence:

> Tomorrow when they turn ash,
> the steely glint of the stubborn teeth
> will to the festival flash
> the defiance of the bayonet
> at the ready, mocking the sun. (6-10)

The sun here represents the moral, ethical and cultural basis of a people or a nation. To mock it is to undermine the cultural values of the society. The tragic dimension to this poem is that it is not foreigners who are "mocking the sun" but owners of the land who ought to treasure and uphold her values. This process of decadence is, to intensify the tragic tenor, what they call "the sweet things" which becomes the paradox that is central to the poem through which Enekwe indicts not only those, especially the younger ones, who participate in this process, but also the adults who condone this process in society.

"Mammon Worship", "Dictatorship"

In "Mammon Worship" Enekwe turns his attention to corruption at governmental level and takes a swipe at these "rogues" of our society. The poem is a graphic display of the corrupt-rich in Nigeria. The central idiom in the poem is materialism. From that perspective, the poet advances a thesis that centres on the greed of a people who have lost moral and ethical values in the face of overwhelming social immodesties and irregularities. The people satisfy their greed not in the legal, civil manner but in the running infamies that seethe the land. It begins with the other-reflexivity that offers the poet the latitude to distance himself from a class he considers shameless and wanton. It is "they", separated by a widening gap, differentiated by their gross indignities, and mortally condemned to a degenerate life.

An underlying paradox in this poem is the sense of insecurity which rabid materialism brings upon a people, a nation. The poet offers a ground for this where he links riches with what he calls "blood money" (3), perhaps implying that it is on the blood of the innocent that the rich have built their wealth. The hidden message in the juxtaposition of wealth and "blood money" is the resultant nemesis that confronts a greedy clan bereft of all humanity. While they possess "palaces of granite" (2) which should offer them maximum comfort, they are not just preoccupied with the existential problem of securing their lives and what they have, but also have the task of defending themselves against the unforeseen arbiter in the struggle between guilt and innocence constantly going on in their minds. Consequently, in their palaces of granite, "[r]ed-eyed security dogs /walk around them / to scare off nemesis" (5-7). This prepares our minds for the eventual collapse of a materialistic society. Dogs, whether red-eyed or not, cannot secure the corrupt people and prevent them from coming face to face with their nemeses. The second part of this poem dramatises the eventuality of nemesis where death and merriment further establish the paradoxical twist of this poem in standing, itself, as an arbiter between the rich and the poor in the society:

> Funerals of rich rogues
> are for heavy feasting.
> Beer and champagne are aplenty
> for oily throats and sticky fingers.
> Security dogs chat with chicken bones... (8-14)

Here is the final collapse (in front of "the gates of hell") of a materialistic clan peopled by the few rich in a society seething with poverty.

While the rich in "Mammon Worship" are simply referred to as "they" whose referentiality goes deep into the mortified social stratification common in the Third World, the rich owner of power in "Dictatorship" is "it" with a referentiality that offers a bitter satire. "It" refers to "[a] gross beast /[who] hauls itself across the sky /casting a heavy night over the land" (1-3). The land is thus thrown into fear; and from fear to a police state. All the elements become victims of the beast: the air is polluted by the "rotten tongues" (6) of the beast, which, of course, imply the ample narratives of the beast's teaming sycophants; the water of the lake is "blood-stained" (8) possibly by the senseless killings of innocent people; and the wind is heavy with mourning, perpetual and penetrative. Hopelessness stares the progeny of the poor in the face. They become "sunset-bound /without homes" (11-12). This is one of Enekwe's engaging poems that aptly capture the cause of the decadence that set in after the war in Nigeria.

Enekwe's historicism is a re-enactment of the merciless militarisation of the Nigerian state after the betrayal of public trust by politicians. The condition portrayed in this poem is the condition in which Nigerians lived during the most brutal military regime headed by the late General Sani Abacha. All else stood still for the maximum dictator whose vaunting ambition was to be life president of Nigeria. This beast-figure, a replica of self-destruction typical of a thoughtless people, is historicised almost by all poets and writers in Nigeria. In one of his poems, "Malediction for a Maximum Ruler", Remi Raji imagises the dictator as a "cyclops [who] burnt the State House/or who sprinkled the soil with seeds/of sorrow and irrigated the mind/with threats of self-succession"(32).

"SITUATION REPORT"

With dictatorship, the common people are doomed as the poem "Situation Report" depicts. Here, Enekwe, in explicit terms, dramatises a society decadent and endangered by penury. The poet's blunt language and penetrative depiction gives the reader a sense of hopelessness for a people fated for irredeemable misery. He postulates that "Poverty flows like poison" (1), which bespeak of a destructive penury among a people who should not, perhaps, be in such dire want. The thrust of Enekwe's discourse on poverty in this poem begins from the premise that most people in Nigeria, nay Africa, die because of poverty. In a way, the pitiable mortality rate in Africa can be reduced to poverty in the sense that people cannot afford good food and medication thereby becoming vulnerable to terminal illnesses. In this forthright poem, Enekwe makes a statement that bears the utter despair of a nation whose "Dawn yields not sunshine" (4) as a result of which people bitterly resign their fate to the sunless darkness that has been spread on the land by the dictator. In Enekwe's projection of poverty, nations waste, and people perish for lack of basic necessities.

Surprisingly, Enekwe gives us hope in this poem which deviates from his previous process of historicisation of the Nigerian state. If political poetry or poetry of nationalism is, as Raji says, hinged on "the nationalist imagination" (10), which turns the poet's attention to the reconstruction of a collapsed society, then Enekwe's optimism towards the end of this poem invites us to a dialogue with a new vision for his country. This vision, according to the poet, has its basis on "knowledge, intellection and work" (20) which contrast with the laziness, contentment and rot that the land is burdened with. There is also "love for truth and beauty" (24) which should power the sensibility that seeks renewal and regeneration. The poet's desire is to see his people forge a nation "where the hawk and the eagle can perch, /none displacing the other" (26-27). This is justice and fairness. While the poet's palpable optimism may be infectious, it is valid to argue that, given the decadence already shown, any process of believing in tomorrow will require us to re-assess or problematise the potency of art in bringing about moral and ethical change in a society that is practically doomed like the one Enekwe historicises. It seems clear then that Enekwe's commitment as a poet is to his land, which shows "his grasp and understanding of the interplay of social forces...within his socio-political reality" (Nwankwo 27). His poetics, perhaps audience-driven, relaxes the toughness of poetry and charts a middle ground between stiff syntax and loose prosody. Spilling out of this poetics is the dominant theme of war and decadence couched in a historicism that presents Nigeria as a metaphor for doomed nationhood.

Works Cited

Amuta, Chidi. "Literature of the Nigerian Civil War." *Perspectives on Nigerian Literature: 1700 to the Present. Vol.1.* Ed. Yemi Ogunbiyi. Lagos: Guardian Books, 1988. 85-92.

Asoo, Ferdinand Iorbee. *The African Novel and the Realist Tradition.* Makurdi: Aboki, 2006.

Eagleton, Terry. *Literary Theory: An Introduction.* London: Basil Blackwell, 1983.

Emezue, Gloria Monica T. *Comparative Studies in African Dirge Poetry.* Enugu: Handel Books, 2001.

Iyayi, Festus. *Heroes.* Ibadan: Longman, 1986.

Nwankwo, Agwuncha Arthur. "The Writer and the Politics of His Environment." *Harvest Time: A Literary/Critical Anthology of the Association of Nigerian Authors.* Ed. Onuora Ossie Enekwe. Enugu: Snaap Press, 2001. 27-33.

Obasanjo, Olusegun. *My Command.* Ibadan: Heinemann, 1999.

Okara, Gabriel. *The Dreamer, His Vision*. Port-Harcourt: UP of Port-Harcourt, 2004.

Philip, Nourbese. "Earth and Sound: The Place of Poetry." *The Word Behind the Bars and the Paradox of Exile I*. Ed. Kofi Anyidoho. llinois: Northwestern UP, 1997. 169-182.

Raji, Remi. *Webs of Remembrance*. Ibadan: Kraftgriots, 2001.

– – –. "Interview with Julie Dill and Matthew Schmitz." *Sou'wester*. 2001. 9-15.

5

Shadows of Grief
THE LAST BATTLE AND OTHER STORIES
Ogaga Okuyade

> Today's children
> are like morning flower.
> Touched by the sun,
> they fall down and die
> (Enekwe: *Come Thunder*)

VIOLENCE seems to be an incredible artistic intensifier in African literature. From Thomas Mofolo's *Chaka*, to Chinua Achebe's ground-breaking revolution in *Things Fall Apart*, a text that marks a significant turning point in the evolutionary dynamics of African literature, and right till the present, violence continues to occupy a cardinal position even when it is not the subject of the text. To say that most African narratives are contoured with violence is not to say that Africans are a violent people, or that the geographical space labeled Africa is characterized by violent tremors. It rather emanates from the agitations of the people in their responses to oppression, tyranny and marginality occasioned by the egocentrism and depravity of their governments. However, according to Ima Usen Emmanuel:

> Literary writers have consistently addressed their works to the historical, social, political and economic problems of their societies. African ... writers are not left out except that since they operate in an oppressive system, their works are preoccupied with themes of racism, protest, conflicts and violence. (106)

Physical and textual violence are, therefore, not an African phenomenon, especially since a natural response to injustice and the devaluation of human rights is resistance, often translating into inexplicable violence. Although violence is not a new theme of artistic creation, its complexion in literature continues to alter with the passage of time. Odile Cazenave argues that "the late fifties and early sixties, violence meant colonial violence, from repeated humiliations and denigrations to physical violence and torture for the ones resisting colonial power... " (59). Violence in African literature today has assumed a new dimension. We have noted that this departure from the initial tone and form of violence in recent times is informed by the despoliation of the collective dreams of the African peoples by their governments.

The dissatisfaction of the people continues to create cracks and tensions within the various nations in Africa. The inability of government to caulk the cracks and level the rift between themselves and the ruled has made a violence-ridden slum of Africa. The civil strife which erupts from the resistance and agitations of the people usually metamorphose into bloody civil wars and at times assume genocidal proportions. The loss of faith in government by an alienated people continues to find a looming space in African literature. This category of literature is designated "the literature of disenchantment". Jonathan Ngate describes the phenomenon as the politics of anger: "Disillusioned with the new African republic and the new leaders ...narrators of those novels are much engaged in what might be properly labeled a politics of anger" (59). However, Pacale

Perraudin opines that the animating force behind these acts of violence stems from "a desire to weaken the ability of the other to assert himself or herself within a realm of power that is in the process of being contested" (73).

The subject of this discourse is not essentially to interrogate the essence of graphic representations of violence in Onuora Ossie Enekwe's collection of short stories, *The Last Battle*, because there is nothing poetic about war, as there is no glory in the blatant waste of human lives and property. However, considering the fact that the social experience that has shaped the artistic consciousness of Enekwe is war, how then can the tragedy of war be aestheticized? To put it more precisely in Yves Reuter's terms: "How can we subject what stems from horror to aesthetic judgments?" (18). Chidi Amuta critically indicates how a writer, trapped in the polarity of art and the reality of history, negotiates his/her craft between the poles when he suggests that as war "puts the greatest pressure on human nature, relationships and institutions, it becomes also a fertile ground for the literary imagination" (86). The hub of the discourse therefore, anchors on how one can read texts bordering on violence and make significant the representation or, better still, the relevance of violence in literary texts. In attempting a discourse of this nature, it is imperative to bring to the fore the yardstick of measuring textual violence as history, and that strictly crafted for the pleasure of art. Richard Pribe offers the critical machinery for this measure, when he argues:

> In broad human terms, representations of violence in any literature, as in life, may do one of three things: they may overwhelm us with a sense of the banality of violence, they may impress in us our capacity for the demonic, or they may serve to leave us with some sense of the sublime. The banal, the demonic, and the sublime however, are not easily separated in our daily lives. (47)

From Priebe's argumentation, it becomes manifest that violence is an unavoidable part of human nature or existence and no one has the luxury or exclusive access to it. Besides addressing the relationship between memory and history, and how history shapes the collective, we shall go beyond the sordid representation of horrific violence, which Arlette Chemain-Degrange describes as "Overabundance of Violence Scenes" (15), to examine Enekwe's stories as witness and demonstrate the fact that his stories transcend the mere aesthetic pleasures that art is said to guarantee.

To understand the nature of the representation of violence in Enekwe's fiction, Udumukwu's admonition that "the works which have emerged as a result of the Nigerian civil war, cannot be understood without their specific historical forces..." (169) is of significance. The histories and geographical conditions of African countries vary with different stages of economic development, sets of public policies, and different patterns of internal and international interactions. The sources of conflict in Africa equally reflect this diversity and complexity. Some of the sources of conflict in Africa are ignited by internal feuds, some reflect the dynamics of a particular sub-region, and a few have international dimensions. Regardless of these varied sources of conflict in Africa, most of them are linked with a number of common themes and experiences. Armed violence and conflict in Africa are often caused by issues which range from lack of transparency by the ruling regimes, little or no checks and balances in the system and non-adherence to the rule of law, to the absence of a peaceful means of change, reliance on centralized and highly personalized forms of governance and frequent ethnic domination and conflicts.

The Nigerian civil war had a monstrous ethnic complexion. As self-governance began in 1960, it was evident enough that the units which made up the Nigerian nation were dangling in disunity. Although the amalgamation of Northern and Southern protectorates symbolically represented a harmonization of the ethnic groups, the people could not see themselves as a homogeneous group. But beyond theorizing violence and the historiography of the Nigerian civil war, how does Enekwe represent the Nigerian disintegration and violence in his oeuvre? One thing about which there is hardly any doubt when considering Enekwe on the Nigerian civil war are the varied shades of grief he cartographs and the authenticity of his story. Despite the fact that the sub genre of the short story only guarantees a compressed account of thematic exploration and a condensed plot structure, indicative of brevity because of the confining compass of the short story, Enekwe is still able to give a panoramic view of the Nigerian civil war. Besides the ferocious and visceral descriptions, which create a powerful compelling sense, not only of the chaos, but of the way we build and understand memories, Enekwe's panache for spinning yarns of despondency through his deployment of images and symbols, confronts the human psyche by making textual grief and pain visible even when such pain and grief are not soused or immersed in the imagery of blood as with the first and second stories of the collection.

The Last Battle has ten stories with only five directly connected to the war. The first two stories, "Emente" and "The Minister's Wife", have grief and violence respectively as cardinal issues even when war is not the subject of the stories. The actual stories on the war present us with images of crude barbarity which Enekwe employs to emphasize the perils of violence and war. The blood-soaked earth, the lifeless bodies laying motionless, the cries from the trenches, the broken boots of soldiers, the air raids, the agony of hungry, limbless soldiers, the corpses piled by the road side, the cries of prisoners of war trying to flee the ballistic missiles all seem to confirm the bestiality and ferocity of man during war. As the reader considers the blatant waste of life and property in an abysmal dimension, numerous questions come to mind, one of which is: how can any good emerge from something bleak and so horrific?

The thematic concern of the stories is the colossal destruction engendered by the war. In "An Escape", the moral degeneracy of individuals, particularly women, is artistically captured. The narrative gives a cinematic account of the moral bankruptcy of young Vicky who would do everything humanly possible to survive the vicissitudes of war. The story equally recreates the varying unpredictability of man's conscience. Vicky's character demonstrates the extent people, especially women, can go for the sake of survival. Vicky's latest lover, Major Amah, epitomizes human moral debasement and callousness to the suffering of others. This is what Ezeigbo projects as the most potent cause of the collapse of Biafra. Joe, Vicky's amputee lover has lost a limb in the war. One would expect that people like him should be encouraged and not pitied or jeered. But Joe refuses to be patronized and pitied. He rages at Vicky when he discovers that she has become a danger to his sanity and sense of survival. He rejects her gifts and pity and asks her to leave. Even in the chaotic circumstances of the war, and the anguish and horror that it engenders, Vicky ultimately realizes that she is only a hopeless woman in a war situation, and that her Major lover, who is an uncompassionate opportunist, is exploiting her helplessness and grief. Rather than sit with him in the car and enjoy the ride en route his bed, she insists: "Corporal, please stop, let me off" (79). She grows increasingly restless and as she jumps off a mobile vehicle, the Major could not save her. The sense of heroism Vicky displays reveals that in the frenzy of the moment, individuals sometimes brace up to the challenges of war and chaos.

"Bloodstains on the Sand" and "Dealing with the Enemy"

recount the brutalization of the youths and their initiation into violence which marks their loss of innocence. Although during war, combatants polarize the field of battle and the paradigm of 'we and them' reverberates in their psyche, they forget that the declared enemy could be their next-door neighbour. Enekwe demonstrates in this story that the issue of protecting civilians in situations of conflict becomes pointless when everyone on the other side is branded a traitor and mortal enemy. Chief Okoro and his son, Uzo, are treated with indiscriminate and ruthless ferocity as the Federal troops refuse to abide by universal humanitarian principles. When captured, Okoro and his son are supposed to be treated as prisoners of war but they are murdered in cold blood. The circumstances resulting in their deaths is not combat but the mindless rage of hate which is celebrated in the occasion of violence when the mind has reached its high point in barbarism making pointless the rules and laws of war.

"Bloodstains on the Sand" and the title story, "The Last Battle", dramatize issues unexpected in moments of violence. The stories differ from most short stories on the Nigerian civil war. They explore the relationship between courage and maturity vis-à-vis manhood and heroism. "Bloodstains on the Sand" comes very close to Stephen Crane's *The Red Badge of Courage*. The similarity between the two narratives is dramatized in the acute sense of fear and courage displayed by two characters in the respective narratives. In *The Red Badge of Courage*, Henry Fleming flees in terror and endures a variety of physical and psychological agonies on the first day of battle. However, when he returns to his unit that evening, Fleming finds his comrades willing to accept his lie that he was separated from the line during the heat of battle and that the injury he sustained on the head was caused by enemy fire. Since fear had only taken the better of him in the dark, he reasons that he had only "performed his mistakes in the dark, so he was still a man" (86). He fights fiercely the next day, and his fellow soldiers lavish encomium on him.

In Enekwe's "Bloodstains" the people of Apama evacuate their native homes because of the impending dangers and horrors but Chief Okoro refuses to leave. Instead he takes malicious pleasure in taunting his son, Uzo, simply to establish the fact that the young man is a coward because he is fleeing a home that is about to be destroyed: "Uzo, you have betrayed your manhood. You hear the sound of guns and you quake like a bamboo in the wind ..." (83). Although the old man's manly obstinacy dooms him and his son, Uzo transcends his limitation of fear and becomes a man before the bullets of the federal troop eventually fell him. Uzo initially abandons his father and flees the village with his siblings only to return because of his sense of duty to family and his sense of moral justice. As he runs, he appraises the proximity of an artillery shell to his location and decides to stop. He begins to regret abandoning his father.

> What would their people say ...?
> It would be a terrible disgrace. Yes, he felt, it was what he had feared. His father wanted to die, but with Uzo. His father had lived his own span of life. He had no right to endanger the lives of his children.
> Nevertheless, Uzo was stymied by guilt.... How could one leave his father in danger ...Then he stopped completely, turned and began to move back towards the village. (84-85)

Uzo's decision to return to the village proved a nugatory venture on the surface. It could be described in Zhu's terms as "absurd courage" strictly because such courage "derives from vanity" from his desire not to be regarded as a weakling and failure by the villagers, rather than from the "righteous inducement" of true psychic and mental power (3-4). Considering he reasons for his decision to return to his father, Uzo, no doubt, operates out of vanity by appraising himself only from the perspective of what others may think rather than his own moral sense. The emotion of fear Uzo displays before fleeing and that which he displays on his return have the same intensity. Both behaviours neither stem from what Howard Horsford describes as "conscious, willed intention" (123) nor heroism. But Uzo has only responded to the situation as an individual. To return in order to talk his father out of his narcissistic rage, motivated by the melancholia of exile at old age, is enough evidence of courage and bravery. By returning to his father Uzo attains maturity, because his compassion for his father in circumstances of a life-threatening situation shows that people trapped in a crisis like war could equally display some degree of will power when animated by their own humanism. Though he dies, Uzo has tactically undergone a whole gamut of human emotions and conferred a great degree of growth upon himself. Through the story Enekwe explores the elasticity of courage and maturity, if we consider John Hersey's conclusions that except for the "hard knot which is inside some men, courage is largely the desire to show other men that you have it" (qtd. in Monteiro, 199-200) but courage could exist side-by-side fear or, rather, fear may invigorate an individual in desperate moments.

"The Last Battle" is another story that explores heroism in combat as a cardinal point in Enekwe's narratives. Regardless of the feeling of disenchantment and disillusionment experienced by both soldiers and civilians, some individuals still operate within a spectrum of morality. Army lieutenant Umeh distinguishes himself as a courageous soldier all through even when his superiors are steeped in corrupt practices. He has on several occasions suffered severe injuries from battle with bullets buried in different parts of his body. His sense of patriotism and heroism are commendable. Although Umeh, complains angrily at his superiors for his transfer from sector to sector, he is only frowning at the loss of faith and the alteration of the Biafran ideal with which they were galvanized at the wake of the war, and the subsequent disillusionment resulting from the gradual collapse of those ideals. This issue is vibrantly espoused in the inability of the soldiers to meet the choric end of the songs he raises to spark their spirit.

As the zero hour approaches, Umeh seems unsettled. It is not fear that grips him; it is only restlessness and a heightened sense of things. He already understands the matrices of this uneven warfare. Rather than allow the young inexperienced soldiers under his command go to battle extempore and be annihilated, he performs a rare heroic feat in the face of battle. He had already admonished the soldiers to take their positions in their various fields of fire and await his signal. Paradoxically, when he gives his order, it is that of surrender. This is another act of heroism because his decision to surrender is not borne out of fear or selfish reasons. It is rather a selfless act geared towards salvaging what is left of the Biafran soldier. Unlike Second-lieutenant Umana, Umeh is not willing to risk the lives of his men for the sake of vanity because the boys are already broken in spirit. The act of salvaging life in the intense heat of battle is in itself an act of heroism.

The last story in the collection, "War in the Head" is not only pensive, it is grisly because the tragic death of a student-soldier who manages to survive a war so traumatizing to the psyche of the people is sickening by all standards. The heavy air raids that tore Biafran formations and towns into rubble during the war, and the post-traumatic stress of those raids, are the subjects of this story. The story dramatizes the problems of settling down after chaos. The character of Anthony portrays the endless presence of war in the psyche of individuals involved directly or remotely in the violence. It does not matter on what side one fights; the end of the war is almost meaningless to the inner lives of the people: memories keep intruding so strongly that any return to normal life is almost impossible.

Anthony's existence has been totally damaged. He can hardly find peace; he is haunted by what Benjamin Stora calls "bruised memory" (91). In the story, one notices the death-like numbness clouding Anthony's psyche. This is further complicated by constant nervousness manifested in his restless, uncoordinated movements. Anthony continues to relive the past because his subconscious has been severely battered by the experiences of the war. He is unable to return to the present as he dies with his hope of reuniting with his family. Enekwe gives the reader an opportunity to psychoanalyze post-trauma victims in order to better understand and gain an insight into the experiences of the people without distorting the agony of the victims and the crime of the perpetrators.

Although the question of betrayal, guilt and shame continues to psychologically punctuate the thoughts and memories of those directly involved in the war, it is appropriate and important to explore the traumatizing effect of the air-raid experiences to understand their import on both the people who endured them and the production and reception of literature about them, especially the story "War in the Head" and the novel *Come Thunder* by Enekwe. Both texts become representative sources to study the full import and complexity of the issues of the bombings in the defunct Biafra.

"War in the Head", in particular, offers an interesting literary and systematic approach to the study of Acute and Post-traumatic stress Disorder. Anthony's psychological crisis stems from his inability to dislocate himself from the past and reposition himself in the present. The psychological problem he experiences is a signpost of "an inadequate way of coping with extreme stress" (Kleber et al: 234). Anthony's emotional reactions are so acute that he can hardly recall parts or even the entirety of the trauma. His inability to come to terms with the present makes him experience numbing estrangement, which is responsible for the absence of emotional responsiveness, and which Robert Lifton describes as "psychic closing-off" (127). The trauma experience alters Anthony's cognitive ability, which he manifests in insomnia, feeling of hopelessness and guilt. Anthony's response to the present eloquently encapsulates the three major symptom clusters of post-traumatic stress disorder, which Susane Vess-Gulani enumerates as "intrusion, avoidance, and hyperarousal" (180). Of the three symptom clusters, intrusion is of paramount importance when considering Anthony's uncoordinated response to situations that culminate in the incalculable tragedy of his death. The term "intrusion" is applied to a condition when, involuntarily, according to Padmal de Silva and Melanie Marks, the individual persistently re-experiences the traumatic event in the form of "distressing images, thoughts, perceptions, dreams, or reliving" (Harold Kaplan and Benjamin Sadock 1227). They are often provoked by internal or external cues such as certain "sights, sounds, and smells" (Laurence Miller: 18) which initiate a process of (re)-memory of any part of the trauma. These intrusion symptoms are linked to symptoms of avoidance. Thus the more Anthony tries to settle into the present and return to normalcy, the more his thought process and psychic networking are altered by the intrusion of images of the war. The air raids and bombings leave Anthony and other survivals without a past or future but in a continuous state of inner destruction. This reduces them to living in what Judith Herman describes as "an endless present" (47). For instance Anthony shivers terribly on seeing soldiers emerge from the bushes:

> Early one morning, two days later, Anthony rushed back from the toilet and pointed a shaking finger towards the northern end of the campus. "Look, look," he said ... Momentarily, Anthony fixed his timid, questioning eyes on his roommate, and ran out of the room in panic. (139)

More than a metaphor for the inner destruction of Anthony, the emergence of the soldiers aptly demonstrates that his psychic networking has not only been battered, his visual cortex has equally been altered. Because any image indicative of a signpost of the war does not only create a process of re-memory for him, but brings the past into the present, thereby destroying his natural and psychological development through his hyper active imagination.

The above instances show how Enekwe's fiction reveals the deep and ongoing traumatization of his characters. His symbols, imagery and lucid language create a cinematographic montage which allows the reader get more emotionally involved, not to mourn, but to re-live the experience. He writes in a style compelling enough to leave the reader with questions (s)he must answer privately. The loss of a sense of time, common sense, and history, plays a cardinal function in Enekwe's stories, poems and also his unpublished play, *The Betrayal*[1]. For Cathy Caruth, this 'contagious' nature of trauma has become our only way to gain access to our past in a world that is perceived and labeled as a post-traumatic century (24). Enekwe's oeuvre will finally attract the desired critical attention they should, for he is a writer whose works signpost not only his remarkable achievements and contributions to literary studies but also the collective artistic highpoint of post-colonial African literature.

NOTE

[1] Many thanks to Professor Enekwe who made available his texts, especially, the unpublished manuscript of his play, *The Betrayal*, to me.

Works Cited

Amuta, Chidi. "Literature of the Nigerian Civil War." *Perspectives on Nigerian Literature: 1700 to the present.* Ed. Yemi Ogunbiyi, Vol. 1, Lagos: Guardian Books Nigerian Limited, 1988. 85-92.

Braswell, M. Sean. "War Stories: "

'Truth' and Particulars." *War, Literature and the Arts.* Fall/Winter, 1999. 148-156.

Caruth, Cathy. *Unclaimed Experience.* Baltimore: Johns Hopkins UP, 1995.

–––. (ed) *Trauma: Explorations in Memory.* Batimore: John Hopkins UP, 1995.

Cazenave, Odile. "Writing the Child, Youth, and Violence into the Francophone Novel from Sub-Saharan Africa: The Impact of Age and Gender." *Research in African Literatures.* Ed. John Conteh Morgan. 36, 2, 2005. 59-71.

Crane, Stephen. *Red Badge of Courage. Vol. 11,* The Works of Stephen Crane. Ed. Fredson Bowers. Charlottesville: University of Virginia Press, 1975.

Emmanuel, Ima Usen. "Human Violence in Toni Morrison's Sula." *Uyo Journal of Humanities.* Ed. Chris Egharevba. 11, 2006. 105-126.

Enekwe, Onuora Ossie. *The Last Battle and Other Stories.* Nsukka: Afa Press, 2005.

–––. *Come Thunder.* Nsukka: Afa Press, 1984.

Ezeigbo, T. Akachi. "The Taste of Madness: The Short Story on the Nigerian Civil War." *A Harvest from Tragedy: Critical Perspectives on Nigerian Civil War Literature.* Ed. Chinyere Nwahunanya. Owerri: Springfield Publishers, 1997. 194-207.

Herman, Judith. *Trauma and Recovery.* New York: Basic Books, 1997.

Horstord, Howard. "He Was a Man." *New Essays on The Red Badge of Courage.* Ed. Lee Clark Mitchell. Cambridge: Cambridge UP, 1987. 109-127.

Haynes, Samuel. *The Soldier's Tale*. New York: Penguin Press, 1997.

Izevbaye, Dan. "Naming and the Character of African Friction." *Research in African Literatures*. 12, 2, 1981. 162-184.

Johnson, Alex. "Sunset at Dawn: A Biafran on the Nigerian Civil War." *African Literature Today*. Ed. Eldred Durosimi Jones. 11, 1980. 148-160.

Kaplan, Harold and Sadock Benjamin (eds.) *Comprehensive Textbook of Psychiatry*. IV, 6th. Battimore: Williams and Williams, 1995.

Kirk-Greene, A. H. M. *The Genesis of the Nigerian Civil War and the theory of Fear*. Uppsala, the Scandinavian Institute of African Affair: Research Report No.27, 1975.

Kleber, Rolf, Charles Figley and Berthold Gersons (eds.) *Beyond Trauma: Cultural and Societal Dynamics, The Plenum Series on Stress and Coping*, New York: Plenum, 1995.

Lifton, Robert. *History and Human Survival*. New York: Vintage, 1971.

Miller, Laurence. *Shock to the System: Psychotherapy of Traumatic Disability Syndromes*. New York: Norton, 1998.

Monteiro, George. "After the Red Badge: Mysteries of Heroism, Death and Burial in Stephen Crane's Fiction." *American Literary Realism* 28, 1995. 66-79.

Ngate, Jonathan. *Francophone African fiction: Reading a Literary Tradition*. Trenton: Africa World Press, 1988.

Nwankwo, Arthur A. and Samuel U. Ifejika. *The Making of a Nation: Biafra*. London: C. Hurst and Company, 1969.

O'Brien, Tim. *The Things They Carried*. New York: Penguin Books, 1990.

Ogunyemi, Chikwenye Okonjo. "Introduction: The Invalid, Dea(r)th, and the Author: The Case of Flora Nwapa, aka Professor (Mrs.) Flora Nwanzuruahu Nwakuche." *Research in African Literatures*. Vol. 26, No. 2, 1995. 1-16.

Perraudin, Pascale. "From a 'large morsel of meat' to 'passwords-in-flesh': Resistance through Representation of the Tortured Body in Labou Tansi's La vie et demie." *Research in African Literatures*. Vol. 36, No. 2, 2005. 72-84.

Priebe, Richard. "Literature, community, and Violence: Reading African Literature in the West, Post - 9/11." *Research in African Literatures*. Vol. 36, No. 2, 2005. 46-58.

Reuter, Yves. Introduction. *a l'analyse du roman*. Paris: Bordas, 1992.

Silver de Padmal and Melanie, Marks. "Intrusive Thinking in Post-traumatic Stress Disorder." *Post-traumatic Stress Disorder: Concepts and Therapy*. Ed. William Yule. Chichester: Wiley, 1999.

Stora, Benjamin. "Women's Writing between Two Algerian Wars". *Research in African Literatures*. Vol. 30, N0. 3, 1999.

Udumukwu, Onyemaechi. *Social Responsibility in the Nigerian Novel*. Port Harcourt: Sherbrooke Associates, 1998.

Vess-Gulani, Susanne. Troubled Memories: Post-traumatic Stress, German Writers, and the Bombings of World War Two." *War, Literature and the Arts*, Vol. 17: 1&2, 2005. 175-194.

Zhu, Weihong Julia. "The Absurdity of Henry's Courage." *Stephen Crane Studies*. 10.2, 2001. 2-11.

6

Eco-critical Spaces
Nature in the new Nigerian poetry
Devapriya Sanyal

THIS chapter is a reading of what has been tagged 'New Nigerian poetry' and uses the poetry collections *Marching to Kilimanjaro* (Ossie Enekwe 2005) and *Full Moon* (Chin Ce 2001) – two works made available in PDF format – to focus mainly upon how local poets in Africa perceive nature in their poetry and what possible interpretations can emerge from their poetic representations of personae, subject and ideas with the natural landscape. Interestingly, as Eco-criticism attracts scholarly interest throughout the Eastern and Western hemispheres in the twenty-first century, arguments still abound concerning standards of practice, critical focus and the actual relationships between environment and literature. In a concise summation of the issue, Michael Cohen observes that eco-critical

> ...contention over strategies of representation and the underlying ideologies that create them are likely to provide unending

discussions that no doubt will be shaped by the unfolding of cognitive studies. ("Blues")

While spirited discussions and propositions continue in the West, some eco-critics have been very busy creating "model" nature writings in the tradition of Henry David Thoreau, John Muir, Mary Austin, Aldo Leopold, Rachel Carson, Wallace Segner, Robinson Jeffers, Edward Abbey, Gary Synder, Ann Zwinger, Wendell Berry and Barry Lopez, while others have not been too idle in the narrativisation of scholarship as a method of imparting and exploring knowledge. For critic Lawrence Buell, this foregrounds the "liveliness" and not "consensus" that abounds in critical practice. For him this point of disparity is traceable to the concept of literature and environment. As he states:

> Literature-and-environment studies are anything but unanimous, for example, on the sense in which literary texts can be said to render extratextual environments or on how if at all literary inquiry might be based on models taken from natural science or science studies. ("Letter")

However, Cohen is quick to point out that "because literature is about human expression, all theories of representation must be about human strategies and therefore "anthropocentric". Eco-critics constitute an interpretive community whose works focus primarily on literature, not nature." As he reminds us,

> imaginative writers may not have to ask hard questions about representation and cognition, but critics do. This is why it can be dangerous to follow the practice so frequently found in Ecocriticism, of taking established nature writers to be reliable theorists on nature writing, and of importing their language into the

critical vocabulary. ("Blues")

Our practice departs from those of mainstream Western scholars as described above and situates the investigation on the broadest definition of Eco-criticism as the imagining and representation of nature in literary texts. And so our use of Eco-criticism in this study shall be based broadly on the definitions of the concept offered by Cheryll Glofelty and Michael Cohen. According to Cheryll Glofelty, Eco-criticism

> shares the fundamental premise that human culture is connected to the physical world, affecting it and affected by it. Ecocriticism takes as its subject the interconnectedness between nature and culture, specifically the cultural artefacts of language and literature. (qtd. in Cohen "Blues")

If we approach the poetry of Ossie Enekwe and Chin Ce from the interconnectedness and relationships between cultural artefacts of language and poetry vis-à-vis natural landscapes, spheres and climactic and meteorological elements, invariably then this study becomes an investigation of artistic representations of man and nature, which Cohen recognises when he defines Eco-criticism as an approach that

> focuses on literary expression of human experience primarily in a naturally and consequently in a culturally shaped world: the joys of abundance, sorrows of deprivation, hopes for harmonious existence and fears of loss and disaster. ("Blues" ASLE on-line)

Like Indian authors, such as Anita Desai and Rasipuram Narayan, who chronicle the aspirations and conditions of ordinary people of India, the poetry of Enekwe and Ce share some similarities in their projection of human cultural traits of deep emotions thrust against natural landscapes, seasons, seasonal changes, flora, fauna and other environmental occurrences in Africa. It is the exploration of these sentiments both on a personal scale (as does Ce) and on a larger community scale (as does Enekwe) that informs our eco-critical interest in these contemporary African poets. We shall proceed by seeking and establishing the interconnectedness and relationships between the use of particular nature images in their poems and how these yield a central eco-critical message in the poetry of both writers.

In his *Full Moon* collection of thirty-eight poems, Ce creates a picture of a stoic individual, a lone figure who is undoubtedly on "transit" as deducible from many of the poems. The unknown destination of this movement or "quest" renders the persona's search an endless, if not impossible, mission. Hence like the search for the mythological "Sangreal" by the Knights of the Holy Grail, Ce's persona takes the quest as an end in itself and celebrates the different experiences that he encounters in the course of his travels. Although the thirty-eight poems are all different in themes, yet the celebration of themes, motifs and images acts as a link for most, if not all, of the poems.

THE "I"

Identified as a "journey man," the "I" persona in Ce's *Full Moon* is shown always on a voyage, passing through an unknown destination. However great the temptation might be to conclude that the quest here is for love (and this is a major theme in many of the poems), we may rejected this in the face of textual evidence that notes otherwise. Ce's emphasis is on the idea of travel and the individuality of man:

> And I, traveller of the highway,

> Long for the guiding song. (18)

And in the next poem "Fortieth Avenue" he reiterates:

> And now I have come far away
> In my loneliness... (19)

By this emphasis, the poet puts forward an awareness unarguably on the condition of "loneliness" or "aloneness" which his persona experiences. This idea of "aloneness" is constantly projected against different natural motifs of distance "far away", "truth", "fires", "highways", etc. This situates nature as a co-player, a companion or witness in the different states of loneliness of the persona. It is by constantly drawing these parallels between the lonely individual and aspects of nature that the poet reiterates his message of "Aloneness" as being the constant natural state of man:

> Here on the towering do I strive
> That nothing shall hold my hand... (19)

> Alone in the world's very heart I'll wait
> For the gentle breeze that kissed
> My cheek, (47)

Thus man is essentially an individual unto himself. And even when the persona talks to other characters in a poem, he never fails to remind them of this quality of going within:

> But you stand alone:
> The Fires of Truth
> Guard your endless dreams. (46)

Sometimes we see glimpses of longing for companionship as in "Sweet Reminisce":

> Those days were lonely moments
> drowsing under the wooden shade. (29)

and in "Thoughts of you" the persona confesses:

> Thoughts of you
> gently float around my loneliness.
> ...
> and my solitary wanderings
> carry your lingering presence (39)

But these longings only serve to project the lonely stature of the persona amidst great and profound nature:

> I can see the light of the setting sun
> Streaked across the horizons
> Of never-ending seas.
> ("Sailing" 14)

especially when listening and contemplating intensely,

> Tuned to the puling night
> moon-gazing, collapsing space.
> ("Sweet Reminisce" 29)

A question may be posed as to the poet's projection of a lone individual before awesome nature: Since all of nature, including man, are affective and collaborative, then what must the individual in nature strive for? What fate awaits our civilization if it only alienates nature and finally threatens itself with extinction as in the legend-based poem "Atlantis"? As nearly existentialist or pessimistic as these questions sound, yet the philosophical underpinnings of exercising moderation in human dealings with nature is apparent from an eco-critical reading of Ce's verses. However, this projection is not merely that of an individual that is generally "lost" or awed by nature. A level of synchronicity is achieved between this "alone" individual (who is not really lonely) and the motifs of nature that he identifies with, as in the example above. Hence he describes himself in "Prophecy" thus:

> ... a single eye
> on a mountain range. ("Prophecy" 16)

The identification of the persona with nature is captured on a spiritual level, like in the example above. It is a pointer that a sense of piety is achieved in the reign of poetic imagination and invariably leads us to the theme of celebration of undying spirituality in the one who attains oneness with nature and being. Thus Walt Whitman's persona in "Song of Myself" probably inheres in the idealistic hero of Chin Ce's "This Side the Sphere":

Whitman:
The earth good and the stars good, and their adjuncts all good.
I am not an earth nor an adjunct of an earth,
I am the mate and companion of people, all just as immortal and fathomless as myself,
(They do not know how immortal, but I know.)
("Song")

> *Ce:*
> And there, on the mountain peak
> I have touched
> The summit of dazzling light. (47)

Here, perhaps, is another celebration of the individual, but not on the landscape of physical achievements. It is the possibility of the surviving entity alongside mother nature that would recant extraneous detractions from the goal of oneness with nature and being. As Swami Prabhupada remarks, "both the consciousness of the Lord and that of the living entity are transcendental" (14). Thus one's humanity begins when inquiry is awakened in one's mind and so "every activity of the human being is to be considered a failure unless he inquires about the nature of the Absolute" (7).

On his part, Enekwe offers a panoramic vista of experiences by different people at various places. The "I" in many of the poems in *Broken Pots* and *Marching to Kilimanjaro* is perceived as the "voice" of a narrator or an observer who comments on the incidents he has witnessed. Thus the occurrence of "I" is quite rare. However in some poems, the poet identifies with the persona and assumes the "I". In "Agbogho Mmonwu" the persona identifies himself with the maiden spirit of the dancing mask as a redemptive factor in a premeditated rebellion:

> Let my naked body
> bathe in a fount of melody
> and I shall drop
> this pack of stones.
> ("Agbogho Mmonwu" 2)

The Nigerian award-winning poet Niyi Osundare, described as a poet of beauty and "larger therapeutic importance" (Eke 92), explains this relationship with spiritual nature thus:

> if Okigbo makes supplication to Mother Idoto, Enekwe bends both knees before Agbogho Mmonwu; if Okigbo's own guardian-angel is a "watery presence" Enekwe's is a "dancing jewel." (*Kilimanjaro* vi)

The poet's discomfiture with the "city" that embodies civilisation as a metaphor for corruption is evident:

> I fear that the stony colour
> of this mighty prison
> will sink and cling
> too deep in my soul.
> ("Too Long in the City" 17)

This "fear" stems from the notion of the city as a place of social decadence and degeneracy:

> I ascend you today
> as you swallow in the sun setting
> ...
> I see on your elephant world
> cataracts in your bosom
> ...
> I see within your flanks
> neither love, nor flower or bird
> only broken mud, gaping ("Shock" 6)

The individual cannot compete with extreme materialism which the city maintains as a prerequisite for members of the class:

> I wait to be rejected
> at a spot where my coins only
> could freely admit.
>
> ...
> I think of the journey home,
> of endless trucks slugging to and fro.
> ("Lagos" 5)

Moreover, it is a place where modern youths have mislaid their compass in life.

> I remember Cindy
> who arrived Saturday
> and departed Sunday
> ...
> she rolled along
> in search of peace
> gathering the world
> yet travelling light.
> ("Mandatory Song" 13)

In some of the examples above, we see the downbeat of the cultural landscapes of the city like: "mighty prison", "coins", "days of the week", "Saturday", "trucks", "cataracts" etc. Only a few times does the persona celebrate love and personal relationships:

> I've passed through your threshold

relished its lovely sounds and smells

> Here I set the drums of Obunenu
> for we are one
> in this glorious dust of eternity
> ("Ekene" 22)

In such references we can see the projection of nature images in the use of traditional African drums, "obunenu", and the idea of oneness captured in the image of "dust of eternity."

NIGHT

This is another interesting part of nature that most poets have explored. For Ce's shamanistic stance with poetry and his oracular judgement of posterity,[1] Night is neither good nor bad. It is represented as one significant and powerful domain of nature as we see in the poems "Waiting":

> Soon it will be night
> when the sun goes down
> and the wind brings
> stale gusts from the sea ("Waiting" 26)

and "Sentry Song":

> Now the drumbeats in the night
> Toll the hopes of time's long lives
> (17)

and also in the poetic revelation of that mythological civilisation called "Atlantis":

> Even as the last vision of a desperate leg
> was blacked out in one yawning night. (73)

Hence the need to "chant down the night /and wake the dawn…" (59), in honour of the earth, and of the time when humans can participate actively in daily existence. However against the backdrop of our relationship with night, there are other functions of Night; there are interpretations from which we see night as a metaphor for joy. For instance we perceive "Night" as an opportunity for another phase of experiences for which the persona would gladly yearn but which are impossible during the day. Thus Night is a time to indulge in pastimes of deep dreaming:

> I'd sail all through the night
> Dreaming dreams within my heart.
> ("Sweet Reminisce" 29)

It also offers the opportunity to

> Let the wind carry the voice
> through the deep and silent night.
> ("Sentry Song" 17)

This is a very important time and phase of existence because for the persona it offers opportunity to dream, to long and ponder:

> joyfully
> I feel the radiant light
> Halo over my head. ("Night" 23)

> Each night have I wandered
> in this thicket of my mind
> …
> Each nightly did I thirst
> like a lost faraway lamb…
> ("Night Time" 37).

Even more importantly, it is the time and moment for realizing ideas of beauty:

> The night is the dawn
> of your never-ending love
> as it comes …
> ("Night" 23)

Thrilled by these dreamlike reminiscences and ecstatic realization, the persona follows and admires the coming of the moon, another nature image, into his world of dreams:

> You brighten…
> my night with your luscious gazing…
> ("Queen of the Night" 62)

hence the final tone of regret in the brief presence of this elemental being:

> Ah gone so soon your beauty
> O queen of the darkly night! (63).

This regretful feeling for nature can be noted as two-pronged: the beauty of the moon lasts but little, and the night itself does not last either. For the poet this is but a brief interlude in a dream projectile.

Contrastively, for Enekwe, "Night" is a metaphor of doom. The idea of man struggling against great odds in the drudgery of survival in modern cities (factors that drain his survival impetus) is communicated through the tension between darkness and light:

> night after night
> ready to fight through death
> for grain of fight.
> ("Homeless in the City" 39)

The futility of the struggle is projected as stumbling along the road:

> He stumbles along city streets
> stumbles through alleyways,
> until madness mercifully claims him. (39)

The protective cover of the night is perceived as offering a philistine opportunity to perpetrate the primitive cycle of the food chain.

> Big fish eat snake fish
> Big men small men
> in the belly of the night.
> ("Big Fish" 35)

Thus Night is not evil but its constant association with evil, illness and pollution renders it an obnoxious aspect of nature. To further highlight this feeling, Enekwe attempts to paint two contrasting landscapes – the rural and urban. Between these two prongs, light (signifying good) and darkness (Night, signifying evil) are constantly projected and played out in the universe: "light and dark clash in the lagoon" (35).

> In search of accommodation
> the injustice of the night
> gallops at dawn.
> ("Zaire" 49)

> in the dark city of the dead
> on lonely streets
> dogs bark at crawling shadows
> ("After the War" 41)

> rolling our drums
> all day
> all night long
> to the rhythmic fall of tyrants
> ("The Hill Called Freedom" 54)

> In the dead of the night
> a mating of witches and vultures ("Before the War" 40)

"Witches" and "vultures", African and Asian symbols of evil and decadence, contrast with highly revered agents of light, like sun, thunder, and lightning, to posit the constant opposition of the elements. This brings us to another important product of nature perceived in the poetry of Enekwe and Ce – the sun.

THE SUN

Both poets make references to the sun in their poetry. Ce personifies and endows the sun with godly attributes as in the following references in "Sailing" and "Waiting" respectively:

> ...I can see the light of the setting sun
> Streaked across the horizon
> Of never-ending seas. (14)
>
> it is five and still
> the sun lashes its frenzied tongue
> to sear my blue face. (25)

The sun reflects the poetic moods of the poems and we see the elements having the ability to enforce upon the emotional conditions of the persona further pain, longing and frustration:

> And if the sun shall scorch
> the earth with howling
> windstorms and desert dusts ("A Prayer" 28)

> The sun relentlessly frowned
> Down on the scorching earth
> ...
> Till the sun had long receded
> Toward the Western skies to snore
> Behind her darkened drape.
> ("Sweet Reminisce" 29)

What we encounter in the above examples is mostly incidents of transferred epithets where the poet uses the sun to show varied moods and responses. While the first example explores the traumatic state of the poet-persona, the last two examples display his sense of resignation. Sometimes the sun is used as a metaphor of hope, as in the poems "A New World" and "The Call":

> The eye of the sun shall
> > Calcify the dream. (20)
>
> I shall forge along to build my dream
> On the hill beyond the rising sun. (15)

In Enekwe's poetry the "sun" is a more forceful suggestion of potency and human valour. Regularly does Enekwe use the sun as a positive force for restoration and restitution in an otherwise deteriorating social situation.

> When the sun will darken
> and grow cold?"
> ("Power" 34)
>
> One day, a brush of sunrays
> shall sweep away all this
> ("Songs" 19)
>
> Neto crawled through the womb of isolation
> into the firm sunshine of war
> ("Neto" 53)

The poet's use of the appellation "sons of the sun" (44) for the liberating warriors that shall restore order in a corrupt and polluted continent is an ancient symbolism that has roots in the Egyptian ancestry of the race. This might prove why, in his poems, Enekwe finds solstice in the sun as a means of announcing hope: "Sunset glitters in /a basket of gold" ("Love" 16).

CONCLUSION

Ossie Enekwe's ecological landscape would bifurcate into two dominant worlds – the urban culture, communicated both as subject and image, and the rural world represented by nature. Into these two worlds has man been thrust and compelled to survive. The underlying activity is one of strife and struggle. His metaphors for "civilisation" are downbeat while those for rural life are mostly upbeat excepting some instances in the use of "night" and fauna images ("hawk"). Enekwe parades a plethora of nature objects in *Kilimanjaro*: "birds", "lion", Iroko", "rain", "sun" "earth", "dust", "Mmonwu", "wind", "wave" and "star" etc. These survive as stock motifs about nature. For instance, "Night" achieves a harmful undertone as a result of its cultural association with evil. This is a highlight of Enekwe's poetry which, in all uses and references to Night, does not succeed as something else. Conversely, the sun is a metaphor for light, or the source of life as the ancients of Egypt had meant it. The use of nature images in Enekwe's poetry finds justification in Mwangi's assertion that "liberation African poetry invokes nature to foreshadow the revolution that will rock the continent when the oppressed masses rise up in arms against the oppressor" (*ASLE*). There is no doubt that Enekwe's *Kilimanjaro* falls under the category of "liberation African poetry" with its expression of hope of redemption of Africa from oppressive conditions of neo-colonialism and western capitalism. As he states:

> To fight is to think
> to walk, to smash through
> barricades of injustice
> to tear off heavy chains
> around the mind
> to die into birth

> with the brightness of sunflowers.
> ...
> the struggle spreads
> through the vast territories of combat
> blasting the edifices of oppression...
> ("Songs of Freedom" 61)

Indeed this is poetry "that weaves the natural environment into its themes to enhance the cognitive and political values of images of African natural environment" (Mwangi ASLE). For Enekwe, the African natural landscape is as political as its cultural landscape and this has informed his use of nature images as tropes that survive mostly as stereotypes.

Chin Ce, on his part, weaves a natural ecology where the individual and nature work in a synergy of existence and transcendence. His is the monism that is justified by a wholistic vision of man and nature in varying moods and shades of mystical existence. With the "Journeyman" and "Traveller" he forges through life, gathers experiences, and, above all, relishes the different conditions of being – alone, in love, out of love, in pain, dreaming, etc. Here nature is the valourous co-player in the journey of life. This is evident from the poet's consistent evocation of nature: fire, sun, moon, dreams, wind, clouds, water, stream, air, mountain, lands, soul, lightning, earth, and man. Nature is the constant companion of man in all spheres of awareness.

In Ce's moon and sun, therefore, nature is not merely anthropomorphised (Eke 127); it is, in major parts, transcended in all its complexity. This we can see in the delineation of different ideas of "night" as shown in this chapter. Hence "night" is complex and natural in its uplifting and depressing connotations. Other times the persona's mood is interwoven with nature and we can see in the poem

"Make a wish" the persona imagising the union between him and the beloved as that of sun and stream:

> ...the little stream
> catches the light of the sun
> in a bright union
> (and we'd make our bed
> with these leaves). (30)

Next the poet equates the rhythm of this love with the movement of the waters:

> the water murmurs
> in little ridges
> and flows in the rustling bushes
>
> like the water plants
> we'd rock on the leaves
> ...
> the leaves are swaying tenderly
> (two hearts clasped)
> in the silent flowing stream. (30)

This longing to "make our bed/with these leaves" expresses the unity of the subject with nature. As Eke avers of Ce's poetry, "the functioning of nature and mind is for the poet the ultimate theme of poetry; in his poems the phenomenon actually receives its consummation" (193). Yet this engagement should also be seen from its spiritual dimension where man via imagination is shown to possess all the capabilities of nature – to soar on mountain tops, travel through great distances and through time in expression of self or essence. And so where Enekwe's poetry laments the paucity and limitations of man as a social creature, with nature and humanity projected as political beings, Ce's poetry strives to uplift the individual to share in an idealism of immortality which the spiritual consciousness bestows upon man and nature. His is the dawn of a new realism of timeless shifts and movements within nature through the ages in search, perhaps, for ultimate perfection.

NOTE

[1] See Hamilton's comment on Ce's "most enigmatic poem" entitled "Oracle." The idea of "poet-as-oracle who has the ability to regard features of the world that others pass by unwittingly (2006:114) could also mean the poet as an embodiment of the animism of African religious responsibility to land and nature. This is equally enshrined in ancient Hindu metaphysical landscape where Shamans are an important part of the culture of communal healing and communication with the spirit world.

WORKS CITED

Buell, Lawrence. "Letter." A Forum on Literatures of the Environment. Modern Language Association of America, Oct 1999. ASLE Online, 1999. 26/6/2008.

Ce, Chin. *Full Moon*. Enugu: Handel Books, 2001.

Cohen, Michael. "Blues in the Green: Ecocriticism under Critique." Environmental History 9.1 (Jan 2004): 9-36. ASLE Online, 1999. 26/6/2008.

Eke, Kola. "*Songs of The Season:* Osundare's Lamentation for the Dead and Living." *African Journal of New Poetry*, Vol. 1, V3, 2006. 77-93.

– – –. "'Closer to Wordsworth': Nature and Pain in Chin Ce's Full Moon

Poems." *Critical Supplement (A) 1. The Works of Chin Ce*. Ed. Irene Marques. IRCALC, 2007.

– – –. "Full Moon: The Romanticism of Chin Ce's Poetry." *African Journal of New Poetry*. 4. 2007. 123-139.

Enekwe, O. O. *Marching to Kilimanjaro*. Nsukka: Afa Press, 2005.

Glofelty, Cheryll. *The Ecocritical Reader*. "Blues in the Green: Ecocriticism under Critique." Michael Cohen, Environmental History 9.1 (Jan 2004): 9-36. ASLE Online, 2004. 12/06/ 2008.

Hamilton, G. A. R. "Beyond Subjectificatory Structures: Chin Ce 'In the season of another life.'" *The African Journal of New Poetry*. 1 V3, 2006 95-117.

Mwangi, Evan. "Nobel Prize: A shot in the arm for African Eco-Criticism." *The Nation*. Nairobi, 24 October 2004. ASLE Online 2004. 12/06/ 2008.

Osundare, Niyi. "Foreword." *Marching to Kilimanjaro*. O. O. Enekwe, Nsukka: Afa Press, 2005.

Prabhupada, Swami Bhaktivedanta A. C. *Introduction to Bhagavad-Gita*. California: Bhaktivedanta Book Trust, 1993.

Whitman, Walt. "Song of Myself." *Leaves of Grass*. W. W. Norton <http://www.wwnorton.com> 1973, 12/8/2008.

7

Post-colonial Power Tensions

IN CURRENT WEST AFRICAN POETRY
Ama B. Amoah

THE Postcolonial discourse, being that which attempts "…to elucidate the function of cultural representations in the construction and maintenance of "First- /Third-world relations" (Said 349), adopts a perspective that is constantly aware of power tussles and strategies for "negotiating with the structure of violence imposed by Western liberation (so as) to intervene, question and change the system from within" (350). The negotiation of power, both on political, economic and socio-cultural spheres, and its straggling motifs of social disequilibrium, hybrid cultures, high criminality, prostitution, gender inequality, et cetera, has provided the critical tandem that post colonial discourse in Africa must ally to. This has been the preferred creative perspective of many contemporary African writers among whom Ossie Enekwe, Kofi Anyidoho, Chin Ce and Joe Ushie are significant voices. As Okafor avers:

> A work of act is never created in a vacuum, it mere supposes a culture, a civilization which is the emanation of a particular historical, geographical, socio-economic and political

circumstances hence geography, history, economics, politics are to a great degree ... are indeed very important. (105)

This exposition of recent poetry from West Africa aims at reviewing existing power tensions in different social and political contexts of the African continent. It purveys poetry's attempt to artistically subvert these structures for the enlightenment and empowerment of the people. For the purpose of this discourse, a single poem from each of their selected poetry anthologies shall serve to illustrate how poetry has been deployed to undermine the favourite accompaniments of colonialism, western imperialism and postcolonialism in Africa.

Anyidoho Kofi is the poet from our homeland of Ghana who shares the belief of his compatriots in committed art. His poetry has appeared in journals and anthologies world wide. His three books of poetry: *Elegy for the Revolution* (1978), *A Harvest of our Dreams* (1984), and *Earth Child* (1985) all show sentiments rooted in the traditions and culture of the Ewe. Although Kofi's poetry is wont to be elegiac in tone, it also reveals an artistic awareness of the African universe which situates life and death as a continuum of existence while sorrow and joy occupy the same revolving axis.

"SOUND AND SILENCE"

Underlying Anyidoho's poetry is a sense of righteous indignation at the exploitation, brutalization and dehumanization that he perceives as the hallmark of European colonization of Africa and her peoples. There is anger at the banal ineptitude of most post colonial African leaders. Kofi Anyidoho's "Sound and Silence" explores this social realism with a view to sensitizing people on the dangers surrounding them. He says:

Because because I do not scream

> You do not know how bad I hurt
> Because because I do not kiss on public squires.
> You may not know much I care
> Because because I do not swear again and again
> You wouldn't know how deep I care
> You keep saying
> How some how our world give away
> Doing time in pursuit of signs
> Deprived of all meaning
> And of all purpose
> We break our world in two. Then we
> Split each half into sounds and silences.
> (qtd. in Johnson et al 15)

It is a poetic examination of our modern reliance on physical accoutrements as a means of verifying truth and depth of emotion. The persona sees these outward signs as expressions of insincere feelings, suggesting that a conscious attempt to reflect true feeling in signs is often futile because such signs may fail to convey the desired meaning. It is mere hypocrisy to place total credence on signs for the consideration of human feeling or behaviour since human beings value appearances more than the inner aspect which the eye cannot see. Where much value is attached to what is heard than what is perceived or felt, this has been to the ruin of many nations. It is this human overwhelming reliance on outward manifestations that the poem addresses. The poet persona laments that people do not value his inner state of mind but judge him on his outward appearance. As a metaphor for Africa's social predicament, this poem exposes Western aids and pledges to the continent as pretensions which do not address the real problems of Africa.

Anyidoho's voice poem contends that the meaning and purpose

of human beings do not reside in signs. The subjection of human behaviour to signs is perhaps a further manifestation of an inward deception. Such a belief also goes to great lengths to rip the "world in two": those that believe in "sounds" and those that believe in the "silence". Why is the world is so much interested in signs?

> ...some how our world
> Must live by signs
> But see how much we
> Give away
> Doing time in pursuit of signs
> Deprived of all meaning
> And of all purpose (9-12)

Our evaluation of this poem reveals Anyidoho's underlying concern with issues of love and affection. He carefully registers his impression about the nature and fate of a relationship that is based on outward appearances. The metaphoric title 'sounds and silence' foreshadows the major preoccupation that points at the paradox of life especially in human relationships which shows the differences of human beliefs: "Then we break our /World in two" (11).

Just as literature has the capability of ridiculing society constructively, with the objective of providing solutions to its problems, Kofi Anyidoho portrays the social problems surrounding love and affection which, according to him, is based on 'sounds' and 'silence'. He goes ahead to prove that a display of mere sounds in love could be deceptive. Because they are "deprived of all meaning /and of all purpose" (11). There is a rhythm which attends traditional chants and invocations and which makes the poem sonorous. The repeated 'because' emphasizes the persona's disappointment at serially failed attempts. It emphasises the lack of comprehension of the meaning and significance of silence. Although the language is simple, yet there is a kind of internal modulation that regulates the cadence of thought and meaning. The cryptic structuring at the end of each line reflects a syntactic arrangement common with invocations. There is a break in the flow of thought at line 7 which has only three words. This marks a change in the direction of the poet-speaker's thought as he begins to resolve the doubt expressed in the previous lines. In subsequent lines the poet speaker begins to state the reasons for the doubts. For him, it is because we live by signs which have neither meaning nor purpose that we have our world broken into two. There is sadness in the poem observable from the speaker's tone of despair. The poet speaker's vision is for a united world devoid of hypocrisy and pretension. Once that happens, the "screams" and "hurts" will cease while the meaningless "sounds" will give way to appreciable "silence" of happiness and laughter.

"MANDATORY SONG"

O. O. Enekwe is an important writer whose poetry since the first published *Broken Pots* (1977) have been praised for their "power and forcefulness", and their "roots in genuine emotion." (Ihekweazu iv). Here the Nigerian poet and theatre scholar in "Mandatory Song" (*Marching to Kilimanjaro* 2005) focuses on the social problem of visionless African youths and the predicament of their survival in modern cities. The difficult landscape through which our modern youths have to meander and survive is captured thus:

>   we grope in a dark rout
>   with its plenitude of smoke
>   leaking fuel and mustard. (13)

It is a situation that seeks to annihilate any meaningful existence and growth for youth. Like Kofi Anyidoho's despondent persona in the previous poem, Enekwe's persona is afflicted by the physical predicament of collapsing social structures. This is captured in the paradox of "a burning winter" and the logical need for the youth to escape:

> the youth flee
> the damp walls of home
> roll downtown
> through hell
> in search of fleeting contentment. (13)

Ironically they fly into greater danger. It concurs with the other portraiture of Ce's rebellious youth in "Prodigal drums" who rebels in his protest against work at home: "those killing trips to farm" (40). Here, the youth's lack of awareness and social commitment is reflected in his search of "fleeting contentment." This visionlessness is echoed in the next stanza where the persona, a female equivalent of this state of restive life, is on the edge of a precipice:

> I remember Cindy
> who arrived Saturday
> and departed Sunday
> moving ever onwards,
> in her hand a linen bag
> full of memories. (13)

The notion of restlessness, or better, flight, is conveyed through the imagistic action of "flee(ing)", "roll(ing) down town" and our "Fleeting" Cindy, "who arrived Saturday /and departed Sunday /moving ever onwards" (13). It is this idea of constant movement towards no destination that foregrounds the idea of a restive and visionless youth. This is again achieved through the comparative expression that we witness in stanzas four and five.

> The youth flee
> ...
> roll downtown
> ...
> in search of fleeting contentment. (13)
>
> ... Cindy
> who arrived Saturday
> and departed Sunday
> moving ever onwards. (13)

In the next stanza the movement, as of a perambulation, is synchronized with that of another female youth in the fourth who also rolls along:

> she rolled along
> in search of peace
> gathering the world
> yet traveling light. (13)

The preponderant restlessness and directionless is revealed through the range of Enekwe's diction: "route", "smoke", "flee" "roll downtown", "Fleeting" "arrived" "departed", "moving onwards", "rolled along" (like a rolling stone), "world", "traveling light", "grope", "dark", "smoke", "leaking", "burning", "damp walls", "search" and "fleeting contentment". The poet's diction also connects the idea of fullness with richness although constantly subverted by external circumstances: "human dignity", "plenitude", "mustard", "home", "contentment", "full", "linen bag", and "peace". Having sustained his thematic idea through the collocation of words, he makes it obvious that the predicament of contemporary Africa does not only rest with its socio-historical malaise but is worsened by its youthful loss of vision.

"THE PREACHER"

Chin Ce who wrote "The Preacher" published in *An African Eclipse* (1992) also depicts the lack of genuine leadership and growing youth delinquency in Africa through his poetry. Ce is one among the many who have come to be regarded as the fourth and younger generation of writers from Nigeria. He contributes enthusiastically to the literary debates of the continent with insightful essays on African literature. It is an interesting paradox that Emezue, in her anthology of current Nigerian poetry *New Voices*, includes Ossie Enekwe and Chris Nwamuo, another Nigerian poet, as part of "the new voices of this generation" where Chin Ce and Joe Ushie are said to belong. She writes:

> Enekwe and Nwamuo ..., although having also begun from the seventies, find recurring parallels with the younger generation especially in their assertiveness and resurgence of nationalistic feelings. These qualities have necessitated their inclusion among the new voices of this generation. (10)

These "new voices" do not treat the socio-political issues which lie behind the turmoil of the African continent as an overbeaten theme but make them the centre of the post-colonial discourse. For instance, Ce uses "The Preacher" as his personification of the African story of misdirected youth and stultified power structures in the region. A symptom of the youth's rebellious nature is poeticised *ab initio*: "I groaned as you rose /in robes that greet the floor" (38), while the preacher's unbridled rigidity is streamlined in subsequent lines:

> I watched you ascend
> The sanctity of his sanctuary
> Face straight and bland
> In the calm of Dead sea. (38)

Although the setting is meant to be a religious ground, a church, yet beneath the façade of religion is a tussle, an ongoing struggle between leaders (preacher and his church) and the led (the people who succumb to the preacher's authority). The imagined battle is eked out from the words "agitation", "frenzied", shaking "fist", and the deceptive five-second "calm of Dead sea" before the final explosion: "crescendo of agitation". The wily young take cover under the memory of a heavy meal while waiting out the sermon:

> While my young mind drowsed
> To the steaming stew
> Of the morning meal
>
> I hissed and how I wished
> This consecrated tedium
> Sooner sees its own ending. (38)

The youth's disdain is captured in the gleeful conclusion:

> But hey dear old preacher
> What was that you said again?
> For in my young and vagrant
> Mind, see?

I cannot remember a thing! (38)

The scorn for dubious leaders is again seen in the observation of the actions of the preacher who walks up the altar (Line 1 stanza 2) and preaches in his high-low voice, moving his fist in demonstration of God's power. The poet contrasts the hegemony of religious authority with the rebellion of this changeling. The youngster is portrayed as a silent resistance to the religious and economic exploitation of Africa by her own misguided leaders. Thus the preacher's pretense at holiness is attended by the agitated and ferocious disposition of his gospel delivery. This equally depicts the leader's coercive bid to win the loyalty of the people. It also goes to show that the masses are ignorant of the mission of the leaders or that the generality of Nigerians are ignorant of the evil and selfishness that drive their leaders.

Ce selects casual phrases: "leaves of the book" (not "the Good book" or "Holy Book" as in Western Christian terminology), "lost in the wonderland" (as in a fairy tale), "sketches" (for holy drawings) to show extreme despair for Christian theology while descriptions like "your old and wrinkled face" and "the crescendo of agitation" capture the persona's derision of the preacher. The intimidating unilateral communication of the authoritative preacher is shown in his walk "elephant-like down the steps", and his "face content with completion /of one more divine mission" (26-28). The poet's adoption of rhetoric in the last stanza, "But hey dear old preacher /What was that you said again?(29)" serves as an enquiry into the empty promises of preacher-leaders.

"MOBILE CASKET"

Joe Ushie's "Mobile Casket" from his book *A Reign of Locusts* (2004) is pre-occupied with the problem of Europe's and America's use of Africa for their commercial dump. Ushie is a militant younger Nigerian poet, scholar and political discussant. Since his first poetry book *Popular Stand* was released in 1992 he has not relented from his description of modern African leaders (save few) as "cruel and visionless walking lies and traitors to their own people" (Amoah and Lillet 150). In this poem, he exposes the tendency, under license by Nigerian governments, for "used and discarded" cars in Europe, especially Germany and Belgium, to find their ways through the country's borders as "Tokunbo" or "Second-hand" cars. These vehicles, transmuting as indicators of social status, ironically prove the chief cause of death for many citizens, their "expired" qualities in their home countries prior to exportation into Nigeria, Ghana and Togo notwithstanding. In the first stanza the persona observes the

> Tyred caskets cascading on our roads
> deeds of their occupants sealed
> we cannot peep into their locked thoughts
> nor see their wrapped sweatless skins. (30)

The cars are truly "caskets" to carry their occupants to their untimely death, although the users deceive themselves that they are among the upper echelons of society. This introduces the acute social divide between the rich and poor, arising from the inequitable distribution of wealth in most African states. Such social imbalance, along with its political and economic tandems, is replete *ad nauseum* in many African societies. Described as a feature of post-coloniality, a car, as a status symbol, is a way to pass across a message that one belongs to the world of the 'rich'. Thus the persona observes:

> passing, they giggle at us in scornful silence,
> turn in our direction, brother;

> open your fixed lips
> open your cocooned world.... (30)

However, irrespective of the luxurious ride to the end (death), which the poor also arrives at through suffering and strife, the irony is that we all get there finally:

> we are both dead, O brother:
> you, shrouded executhiefly
> in your tyred casket
> going ... on this one road;
> and we, or our skeletons
> tyrelessly watching you
> as we go clothed in the elements. (30)

A major feature of Ushie's style is his play on words: "Tyred," "executhiefly", "tyrelessly" which achieves ambiguity of meaning and purpose. The sounds of the words give the desired meaning while the graphemes denote the ironies of their implied context. Ushie's poetry sustains his irony by this singular device. "Executhiefly," gives indication of the source of income of the car owner. It is twice ironical that a "thief" parades about with a stolen property, the purchased "car" in this instance, and expects public honour as a wealthy citizen. The watching eyes of the people are not necessarily those of admiration but disdain.

CONCLUSION

We have tried to show that Anyidoho, Enekwe, Ce, and Ushie, through their poetry, interrogate power, class tensions and other issues of African post-coloniality by identifying with "...resistant native cultures, (in which) there is both a stubborn confrontation and a crossing over" (Said 359). Their effort further confirms the assertion that

> much postmodern engagement with culture emerges from the yearnings to do intellectual work that connects with habits of being, forms of artistic expression and aesthetics that inform the daily life of writers and scholars as well as a mass population. (hooks 348)

Amongst their major engagements have been the disparity in distribution of wealth, the loss of vision by leaders and youth, and the hypocritical attitude of the Western world to Africa's socioeconomic and political affairs. Their poetry reveals the commitment of art to society in Africa. This dogged poeticisation of societal malaise, in spite of the seamy tastes of Western literature, places their works on the major lists of post-colonial writings which, borrowing the imagery of hooks,

> bear their past within them – as scars of humiliating wounds, as instigation for different practices, as potentially revised visions of the past tending towards a new future, as urgently reinterpretable and deployable experiences, in which the formerly silent native speaks and acts on territory taken back from the empire. (359)

Works Cited

Amoah, Ama and Mark Lillet with Joe Ushie. "After our 'Obliterature.'" *The African Journal of New Poetry*.4, 2007. 143-172.

Anyidoho, Kofi. "Sound and Silence." *New Poetry from Africa*. Eds. Johnson, et al. Ibadan: University Press, 1996.

Ce, Chin. "The Preacher." *An African Eclipse and other Poems*. Enugu: Handel Books, 1992.

– – –. "Prodigal Drums." *An African Eclipse and other Poems*. Enugu: Handel Books, 1992.

Emezue, G.M.T (ed.) *New Voices: A Collection of Recent Nigerian Poetry*. Inglewood: Handel and Progeny, 2003.

Enekwe, Ossie. "Mandatory Song." *Marching to Kilimanjaro*. Nsukka: Afa Press, 2005.

hooks, bell. "Postmodern Blackness." *Modern Literary Theory: A Reader.* Eds. Phillip Rice and Patricia Waugh, London: Arnold, 1989.

Killan, Douglas et al. *The Companion to African Languages*: African Books Centre, 2003.

Okafor, R.N.C. "Politics and Literature in Francophone Africa: The Ivory Coast Experience." *Okike: An African Journal of New Writing*. Ed. Chinua Achebe. 1983. 105-130.

Said, Edward. "Culture and Imperialism."*Modern Literary Theory: A Reader*. Eds. Phillip Rice and Patricia Waugh. London: Arnold, 1989.

Ushie, Joe. "Mobile Caskets." *A Reign of Locusts*. Ibadan: Kraft Books Ltd, 2004.

8

Children's Poetry
OSSIE ENEKWE AND AGWU UDE
Mirabeu Ngene

CHILDREN'S poetry lies in a distinct and vital field of literary endeavour but has been denied serious critical consideration by scholars unlike the interest paid to adult poetry. According to John Allen, children's poetry involves the "constant enrichment of the child's mental structures and of his environment about himself and his environment" (qtd. in Uwandu 304). Also in a paper presentation, "Children's Literature in Africa: Theoretical and Critical Issues", Nana Wilson Tagoe describes children poetry as a work of the critical imagination, and one that is

> produced largely with child's interest and needs in mind... deals honestly with children, portrays them candidly and in the medium to which they can respond with imagination and pleasure. (18)

There is further agreement among critics that in the world of children's poetry, the poet should be capable of arousing the didactic instinct that imbues children with good values which serve as the mould of consciousness. This is because children's poetry aims at developing and influencing for good the behaviour of the child through positive creative imprints on the child's mind; it also makes him memorize and retain those values that should help him attain laudable goals in life. Barnfield observes that "children's poetry deals directly with the child's meaning, understanding, will, imagination, emotion, person and observation" (qtd. in Uwandu, 304) and goes on to spell out the duty or responsibility of the writer for children thus:

> A writer of children's poetry should be aware not only of his or her... creative abilities but also have in mind, psychology and understanding of the child as well as his particular relationship to language either in the written or oral form. (18)

Sometimes for the poet to predict children's interests, responses and feelings, he has to go back to his own childhood, "listening and experiencing from his world and transforming it in accordance with their particular content and purpose" (18). Thus children's poetry stimulates the imagination, builds up the sensitivity and develops the perceptive powers which help them to grow up in their cultural environment. Tagoe reminds us that "children cannot always know what is good for them, (but) ...the writer's manipulative art determines what aesthetic pleasures and imaginative stimulation they will derive from a particular poem" (20).

Another importance of Children's poetry is that it promotes deeper cultural and social values. It seeks to impart messages of wisdom and enlightenment to the child and reveals acceptable norms of behaviour. Unoh, elaborating on the role of children's poetry, claims that:

> Nigerian children can, and should be helped to, acquire desired

attributes through exposure to ...literature that deliberately exposes, ridicules and condemns evils in our society and seeks to inculcate the value of love, courage, honesty, unity, selfless services, respect for authority, elders and patriotism. (qtd. in Ashimole 85)

There is no doubt that children's poetry, art and literature all over the world could be the great custodian of the heritage of symbols essential in making children adore the world they live in. It is an imaginative discipline that helps children to project themselves beyond their own immediate conditions into a range of diverse emotional, political, religious, moral and intellectual encounters that they might have already sensed but which they must be free to experience imaginatively (85). Hence children's poetry does not only give pleasure and entertainment but also helps in affecting positive changes in the society.

Two Nigerian Children's Poets

Ossie Onuora Enekwe and King Agwu Ude belong to the contemporary generation of Nigerian poets who bring positive contributions to bear on current writings for the child audience. Enekwe from Eastern Nigeria is poet, playwright, novelist, short story writer and critic in a bundle. He is a highly acclaimed writer whose works, such as *Igbo Masks* (Literary Criticism), *Broken Pots* (a collection of poems in which the poet struggles with experience of Nigerian disunity and war), *The Last Battle and Other Stories*, (a short fiction collection in which he deals with the traumatic experiences of the Biafran war), *Come Thunder* (a novel also on the war), among others, have earned him national and international recognition. *Gentle Birds, come to me* is his latest collection of poems for children.

King Agwu Ude is also an Eastern Nigerian poet, critic and literary researcher. The charm, lucidity and uniqueness of his works lie in the beautiful blending of two forms of literature, oral and written, still thriving in Africa. His works include the epic tale of *Ina Aja* from his Edda community, *Smiling Through Tears*, (poetry), *The Bitter Pill* (a novel), *Edda Heroic Poetry* (Oral Literature) and *Going to School*, a collection of poems for children.

Both Enekwe and Ude understand the need for children to appreciate poems about their environment and about subjects that fit well into their experiential domain. It is no overstatement that the collections of poems under study, *Gentle Birds Come to me* by Enekwe and *Going to School* by Ude, are richly geared towards stimulating and widening the African child's imagination and vision. Thus these poets do not just compose poetry for children; they go further to impart significant vision and purpose in the child reader's mind thereby urging them on as purposeful extensions of the world they describe. Achebe and Armah see such a vision for society as the realization of infinite possibilities and responsibilities in overcoming evil for the attainment of an ideal and egalitarian society (qtd. in Ihiegbunam 99). For Ihiegbunam, a writer's vision is his contribution to the kind of human society or individual that he believes in (98). And for Wole Soyinka, the writer's vision is "an inner light unavailable to the masses of his people (which the writer) ...should use as his inspiration and insight to guide his society towards a beautiful future" (98).

In a true African sense poetry is didactic and subsists not just for pleasure and entertainment; it therefore contributes to effective and positive changes in the psychology and moral development of the child in society. Children's poetry is thus a product of an enlightened dream to enable the child imbibe good sense, sound judgement and a conscientious vision for his /her future responsibilities. It seems imperative, therefore, that any good poet of children should hold a simple but powerful vision for the child. It is in this regard that Enekwe's *Gentle Birds come to me* and Ude's *Going to School* are relevant to African children and children of the world at large.

ONUORA OSSIE ENEKWE

Enekwe's vision for his child reader is captured in poems such as "Birds, our teachers", "Rainy Season", "Mandela", "Let's Get Together", "Song of Africa" and "Nneka" (mother is supreme). The poems portray human unfriendliness, greed, lack of love, falsehood, lies, war, lack of ambition, and lack of vision as evils that afflict society. In "Birds, our teachers", the poet depicts harmonious coexistence among birds and condemns man's failure to learn from the exemplary life of birds.

> Birds taught humans
> to run, hug the wind
> lift, rise, fly
> and always try. (1-4)

The poem is Enekwe's exposition of the consequence of immoral life in the human world. It may be said that the traumatic experience of the Biafran war lured the poet into writing didactic poetry for children in order to encourage them to eschew tendencies in Nigerian life to "cheat", "lie", or "defy the law". The essence of the poem is that human penchant for wars, lies and deceit should be abhorred. Achebe has stated that "an African creative writer who tries to avoid the big social and political issues of the contemporary Africa will end up being completely irrelevant" (78). It can be seen here that the poets writing for children do not shy away from teaching important historical or social lessons that might help them in life. "Rainy

Season" is Enekwe's attempt to make the child audience know that all sweet things also have some bitterness. The great vision of the poet lies in his attempt to inculcate in the child a healthy, curious, but sceptical, attitude toward life. Furthermore, the poem could reflect the reality of Nigeria's independence which had earlier been embraced with great expectations. The lines, "fill us with cheer" (4), may be said to show the excitement with which independence was received at that time. However, the same rainy season that fills the people with happiness inflicts pains on them: "it will give you cold and lots of pain" (7-8). The opposing side of the rain makes life unbearable and oppressive. The idea of the rain seasons that "fill us with cheer" and the contradicting impression that

> it will give you cold
> and lots of pain. (7-8)

have allowed the poet to capture the realistic situation of post-independent Nigerian society being the failure of leadership to provide for the people, leaving them disillusioned, oppressed and brutalized – the outcome of Nigerian independence. Thus self-rule, which was anxiously welcomed as the beginning of freedom from colonial autocracy and from political and economic enslavement had, as soon as the colonial leaders left, degenerated into massive violence and destruction of lives and property in war because the indigenous extractions proved really no better than the colonial overlords. The poem teaches children to be civil but not servile: "Be not too bold" (5). As a mirror of our society it points to the fact that no work of arts exists in a vacuum. The society creates literature and literature in turn recreates the society.

Enekwe's poem "Mandela" is an ode to the great man of history who fought inexhaustibly for the liberation of his people from the shackle of apartheid and white minority rule. Nelson Mandela is praised for his role as a son of Africa and his dedication to serve his nation: "Mandela, son of Africa fighting for peace" (22-24). The heroic figure of Mandela knows the importance of peace in human relations and fights for it. He has thereby rendered selfless service to his people. Here the poet teaches children determination, courage, humility, freedom and selflessness for their society.

"Let's get together" is a patriotic poem in which the persona calls his group to unite and render patriotic service to the society. The poet persona (speaker) is of the realization that through combined efforts in society, a better tomorrow will be achieved.

> You build your future
> and that of the children
> you create the present
> and the future. (12-16)

In "Mandela", patriotism, unity, hardworking, love and compassion are among the essential qualities for future growth and development, while "Nneka" depicts the supremacy of the mother. The poem encourages the children to love and care for their mother by the virtue of their position in the children's upbringing. "Nneka" portrays how the mother nurtures, caters, trains and provides for them even when there is no hope for the living: "Through her I came to be". The poem preaches love and care for mothers.

The poem entitled "Passing Along" depicts the transcient nature of things, i.e., nothing is stable. Here the vision of the poet is to teach children to make the best use of the time as what they do today determines their future success.

> Yesterday was today

> Like tomorrow, talked about,
> Today will soon be eclipsed. (10-12)

This poem further teaches children about the supremacy of God: "Only God does not change /Only God lives forever" (15-16). This is a striking contrast to the unreliability of human beings who can change at any time.

KING AGWU UDE

The reputation of King Agwu Ude as a visionary for the child reader is established in poems like "Going to School", "Birds of the Air", "Afternoon Rain", School" and "Rose Flower". In "Going to School", the poet teaches the child how to respect and honour parents: "I bow my bye" (3). From the poem children would realize that, in greeting their parents, they have to stoop in respect. The poem also advises children to be courageous, bold and determined in what they do. The speaker puts it thus:

> Like a pillar, I stand
> Marching like a soldier. (6-8)

The persona goes to school and crosses the road with care and alacrity at the same time:

> Left right, left right
> I hasten to my school. (10-11)

And quite unlike the lackadaisical manners of today's students, this poet persona is in a hurry to get to the school on time; while there he greets his teachers and friends.

> Good morning teachers
> Good morning friends. (12-13)

It is rather by the friendly and disciplined attributes of the child poet-persona that the message of the poet is inculcated in the reader.

The poem entitled "School" portrays a common ground where knowledge is acquired. Children are to realize that the school is a place where unity, love, tolerance and mutual understanding in relationships are achieved or established:

> A meeting place
> for pupils and teachers
> a contact spot. (13)

The school is thus a socializing place for children where peaceful interaction and learning are cultivated; in fact a haven "where knowledge is imparted" (10). The didactic content of the poem is that children should be friendly, respect their teachers and schoolmates in peaceable interaction with one another.

"Birds of the Air" is a poem depicting the excitement of birds which give praises to God. This portrays the goodness and worthiness of creation. The birds sing aloud for human beings to know that God should be praised:

> Shout loud your praises to God
> It is good that man should know (5-6)
> That we owe our praises to God. (7)

In "Birds of the Air" the poet depicts the sovereignty of the Most High: "For He is high and we are low" (8). The moral dimension of the poem is that children should know that God is incomparable with man and, perhaps, the supremacy of God becomes a humbling check to the vanity and ambition to rule over fellow men.

In the poem "Afternoon Rain", the poet portrays how a child may perceive the normal course of nature on certain occasions. It is unfair for rain to pour down so heavily in the afternoon: this might indicate nature's cruelty to humans. Thus the child persona advises the rain to fall at night, which is the time when everybody sleeps after the day's work:

> Pour down at night
> While we are all asleep
> You will make our sleep deep
> And our infant dreams sweet. (5-8)

The child's logic goes that if rain falls in daytime it is unfair to him because "mummy" is still at the work place.

> It is unfair if you fall
> My mummy is in the farm
> it will harm her if you fall. (1-4)

In a way the poem is pedagogic as it teaches children not to fall under what a character in a story calls "a useless indulgence to bray at the elements" (Ce *Gamji* 17), but to act responsibly under any situation.

Finally, in "Rose Flowers", the poet portrays the attractiveness of the flower whose thorns do not make for its easy grasping: "Because their thorny stems prick" (4). It tells the child that good things are not easily acquired. However one can afford to pick them if he his determined and wise. The poem is moralistic in teaching children to be wise and observant.

THE STYLE OF ENEKWE'S AND UDE'S CHILDREN'S POETRY

Style is important in communicating the poet's vision. A poet's message cannot be communicated effectively without a distinctive style. It is through style that the poet manifests his vision. His overall view of life is also constantly stemming from that vision and may be determined or hampered in terms of language and imagery communicating the poet's style.

African critics agree that language is an important medium for poetic utterance, a medium with which poets transmit their messages. Lewis Nkosi asserts that a writer's special commitment is to language and its renewal..." (qtd. in Umeh, 21). The effectiveness and vigour of the poets message depend largely on the nature and quality of language. This implies that language is an instrument in the hands of the artiste and how well he utilizes this instrument to achieve his purpose will depend on his capabilities as an artiste as well as on the nature and depth of his vision. Therefore the clarity or obscurity of meaning in Nigerian children's poetry depends, to a large extent, on the poet's degree of mastery of the language appropriate to children. Every poet is conscious of the language of his poetry since language is affected by the poet's audience and message. Some would insist that clarity of expression is important to a poet's good style since poetry could be "an attempt to reach wider levels of meanings, wider spheres of understanding" Ce135). Moreover,

> The language the individual chooses to express ... must communicate in such a way, consciously, that offers the audience ability to understand the impression... as even the best of minds faced with this realization discovers that the activity of expression through language is inadequate to communicate the profundity and intensity of (imaginative) experience. (35-136)

In the same token, Tagoe admonishes that "all writers of

children's poetry should not allow their own taste and preoccupation to influence how the child will react to a particular work"(20). This implies that the language of poetry should be in a style accessible to their psychology of understanding and which enables them to derive aesthetic pleasure and understand the didactic dimension of the poem. Ropo Sekon also asserts that good mastery of the language becomes a source of aesthetic harmony (141). However Umeh claims differently:

> The language of poetry is emotive rather than factual or scientific ...(and) should not be submitted to considerations of simplicity or difficulty ...(but rather) be considered in terms of appropriateness both to its theme (vision) and moods, and to its audience and intention. (111)

In Enekwe's and Ude's children's poetry, nevertheless, one observes that their language has not only explicated but aided their vision for children in their cultural environment. Their language is able to actualise this purpose through the appropriate choice of words as well as the right tone of rendition. For instance, Enekwe's "Birds, our teacher" is rendered in conversational language, and not in a tone that combines with the indifferent or condescending to depict the moral against deceit, cheating, lying, and oppression and war mongering:

> Birds did not teach us to war
> Cheat, lie and defy the law. (5-6)

In "Rainy Season" there is the clear simplicity of the lines "The wet season is here /a period of rain", and the expression, "harvest of grain fills us with cheer" (14) combines with the tone of assurance to convey the relief and excitement which children greet the rain season. But there is need for caution; children should, as the poet informs them,

> Be not too bold
> in the stubborn rain
> it will give you cold
> and lots of pain. (5-8)

This passes on a new note of apprehension. For when the true nature of the rain is shown to sustain the happiness of children, the declarative tone, "it will give you cold/ and lots of pain" (7-8), now reflects the need for temperance that attends the contrary quality of the rain.

In the poem "Mandela", the vigour of utterance reflects the courage and determination with which the protagonist – former South African president Nelson Mandela – had fought for his people's freedom. The language harbours the seriousness of Mandela in fighting to liberate his people. In "Let's Get Together", the imperative tone creates an authoritative voice calling for unity, love and patriotism. The rhetorical question:

> How much do I get from all this?
> How much do you give me?
> How much do I get from all this?
> How much will I get? (48)

comes with a view to debunking the attitude of selfishness in the world of children. In "Nneka", the descriptiveness of the poem reflects the duty and care of children by their mothers. The careful choice of words is to give clarity and rhyme to the poem:

> Though life seems hopeless and grey
> Mother's love shows the way. (7-8)

Similarly the language in King Agwu Ude's "Going to School" conveys the optimism and determination of the various poet personae. The frequent similes – "Like a pillar/ I stand marching like a soldier" (6-8) – further enforce the overall vision of the poem being courage and determination. This seems in line with the critical position that "the language of children's poetry... (should) stimulate children's imagination by evoking associations that enlarge their experiences and...enhance their imagination (Tagoe 21). In "School", the language is descriptive; it vividly paints the nature of school and what it should be:

> A meeting place
> for pupils and teachers. (13)

The poet's use of adjectival phrases tends to elucidate in the child a consciousness of school, and of possible evils in school, as a meeting place, contact spot, social ground, gathering point, special house and clean compound. The descriptive nature of the language is in line with the poet's vision of unity, friendliness, mutual co-operation among the children in a school "where love and unity are grown" (12). In "Rose Flowers", the metaphorical language makes the message clear and vivid in order to help children to gain wisdom knowing that life is full of difficulties and that one requires one's wits to sometimes overcome them. And in the poem "By the fingers that are unwise", the imperative voice reminds children that precious things of life are always difficult to organize. It is evident that not everybody has that wisdom that enables one to acquire it. That is why not everybody succeeds in life. The intimacy evoked by the language: "They are difficult to pick/ Because their thorny stems prick" (24) conveys the message of caution and an attitude of vigilance in the life of the children. In "afternoon Rain", the conversational language combines with a casual reminder: "It is unfair if you fall" (1) to portray the attitude with which the child persona rejects the afternoon rain.

Ossie Enekwe's language has also been shown as appropriate in terms of the message and the audience. As James Reaves states, "it is through language that poetry makes its lasting appeal" (qtd. in Umeh, 291). In Enekwe's "Passing Along", the sun is an image of the good thing just as "kingdom" is an image of greatness, and "God" projects the omnipotence of the supreme being. Ude equally uses such images to bring forth his message of greatness-through-diligence to the child reader. In "Going to school", the "road" is an image of the complexities and confusion that one will pass through in trying to acquire education, while the "pillar" symbolises the courage and determination of the poet persona. The imagery of the "eyes" implies a single vision while "teachers" and "friends" present the school as a ground for formal and social education. In the poem "Rose Flower", the image implies the precious things of life while "thorns" highlight the difficulty and hindrance in trying to acquire them. Images of "Sun" and "Moon" note the complimentary and industrious role of the family in a nation. "Light" implies the happiness which comes as a result of hard work.

Enekwe and Ude seek to artistically arouse the imagination of children by their poetry in a way that reveals their benign vision for the African child in recognition of their position as future leaders, hence the need to weave poems for their moral direction. Enekwe's freshness of language combines with local and national themes to expose the realities of the Nigerian society to the child. The beauty of expression is not even hampered by the use of familiar words and phrases. In his exploration of different areas of Nigerian social reality, he employs poetic devices to put across his vision to the child audience. Both language and imagery in Enekwe's children's poetry reflect the violence, greed, corruption, and other undesirable features of the Nigerian state which poets have demanded their dismantling for a better society. Donatus Nwoga had captured this sense of commitment when he said:

> This type of imagery has reverberations beyond the individual situation…linking the subject and the reader with the connotations of its intrinsic meaning, its social force and its previous usage. (qtd. in Umeh 155)

The Nigerian poet, Chin Ce, also espouses what should concern the poet of nursery verses as "the peculiarity with which familiar themes are expressed (in)…lucidity and lyricism" (38). Says he:

> (children's) poetry can essentially assume the auditory medium of expression which can stimulate greater interest by the virtuous arrangement of verbal and other sound effects, and, at the same time, remain accessible to the sensitivity of the truly younger generation to leave a lasting legacy for the times. (39)

Happily such a legacy for the future is bequeathed our children by Enekwe's poems: proudly functionalist and as politically conscious as they are didactic, and Agwu Ude's poems tending to greater artistic experimentation in its striving to blend oral elements with formal verse.

WORKS CITED

Achebe, Chinua. *Morning Yet On Creation Day*. London: Heinemann, 1979.

Ce, Chin. *Gamji College*. Enugu: Handel Books, 2002.

---. "The Art of the Younger Poets." *New Voices: A Collection of Recent Poetry from Nigeria*. Ed. GMT Emezue. AI: Handel Books, 2003.

Egudu, R. *Modern African Poetry and the African Predicament*. Lagos: Macmillan, 1978.

Emezue, G.M.T (with Chin Ce.) "Critics of the New Poetry." *New Nigerian Poetry*. Ed. GMT Emezue. IRCALC, 2005. 129-155.

Enekwe, Onuora. *Gentle Birds, come to me*. Enugu: Afa Press, 2007.

Ihiegbunam, C. "Vision and Perception: Shared Tradition in Achebe's *Anthills of the Savannah*, Armah's *Fragments* and Soyinka's *The Interpreters*." *Calabar Studies in African Literature: Critical Theory and African Literature*. Ed. Ernest Emenyonu. Ibadan: Heinemann, 1987.

Onyema, Dillibe. "Children's Literature as the Arrowhead of the Next Millennium." *Harvest Time: A Literary/Critical Anthology of the Association of Nigerian Authors*. Ed. Onuora Ossie Enekwe. Enugu: Snaap, 2001.

Skon, Rope. "The Narrator, Narrative. Pattern and Audience Experience of Oral Narrative Performance." *Oral Performance in Africa*. Ed. Isidore Okpewho. Ibadan: Spectrum, 1990.

Tagoe, Nana. "Children's Literature in Africa: Theoretical and Critical Issues." *Children and Literature in Africa*. Ed. Ernest Emenyonu. Heinemann, 1992.

Ude, King Agwu. *Going to School: Poems for Nursery and Primary School Pupils*. Abuja: Pecand Publishers, 1996.

Unoh, Solomon (ed.) *Junior Literature in English*. Ibadan: African

University Press, 1981.

Umeh, Okey. *Poetry and Social Reality: The Nigerian Experience*. Onitsha: Benamax, 1991.

Utoh, Tracie. "Dramatic Parable: Imperatives for Social Change in Post-Colonial Nigeria: A Critical Analysis of Contemporary Plays." *Journal of Arts and Humanities*, Vol. iv. 2002.

Uwadu, Dan. "Child Development through Drama: Dimensions of Children's Drama in Irene Salami's *Short Plays for Junior*." *Journal of Arts and Humanities*. IV. 2002.

9

History and Memory

ENEKWE'S MARCH TO KILIMANJARO
S. A. Agbor

THIS chapter analyzes critical issues relating to the Nigerian society as they rebound in Ossie Enekwe's *Marching to Kilimanjaro*. It examines ways in which Enekwe's poetry opens a range of possibilities for re-interpreting and negotiating the Nigerian, nay African, experience. The aim is to examine the pre-occupations of postcolonial African poetry in a bid to see how they portray the life and ideas of the various societies. Looking at Enekwe's works as reflections of the past and chronicles of the present fulfils one of the functions of literature in any given society to educate by representing and reinterpreting man's diverse experiences through re-memorising.

The literary form enlightens a people's culture because, in the course of writing, the poet uses historical, cultural, language and economic realities of his society as a springboard to his creativity. Chinua Achebe emphasises the role of the African writer as a "watchdog" of his society when he writes that "an African creative writer who tries to avoid the big social and political issues of contemporary Africa will end up being completely irrelevant" (78).

Consequently, a poet uses his socio-cultural, political and historical background to write in a way that his thematic preoccupation reveals qualities of life in his society.

Ossie Enekwe's poetry is set in the context of postcolonial Africa and her many civil wars. The realities of daily living becomes the springboard through which he presents a powerful image of what self-centeredness, injustice, embezzlement and corruption could do in society. He attempts to redefine the relationship between liberation struggles in the social world and the self. Niyi Osundare in the Foreword to *Marching to Kilimanjaro* states that "the thrust of this new collection is the total liberation of Africa from several centuries of slavery and dehumanisation"and that "Enekwe assails this grand project by clamorous reminders of 'the sin of my people/ against my people'"(5). Thus Enekwe's poems are informed by the socio-cultural and political malaise that surrounds his society.

Stephen Greenblatt writes that "history cannot be divorced from 'textuality'" (4). This approach is quite relevant to understanding Enekwe's texts within the context of the history that produced them and the impact they have in re-enacting that history and memory. Dasylva and Jegede, writing on poetry and social commitment in contemporary Nigeria also state:

> Modern Nigerian poetry shows ideological commitment to prevailing socio-political and economic changes... the poems show open criticism of political leadership and support for the masses. The attitude of the Nigerian poets to their subject is due to the role of the poet in traditional society, which has influenced and defined his conception of himself in modern times. The poet takes on the role of prophet, protester and social reformer combining foresight and insight. (140)

We can in this wise analyse the form and content of Onuora Ossie

Enekwe's "Situation Report", "Beggars", "Mammon Worship", "Big Fish Eat Small Fish", "Dictatorship" and "What do you do with all your Power?" One particular insight and constant feature of his poetry is Enekwe's questioning of the continuous suffering of the masses, and the expropriation of national wealth by their leaders. This is seen in "Situation Report", "Beggars", and "Mammon Worship". What seems at stake, above all, is the quest for re-evaluation of national ethic, and the assertion of a common hope. One of the ways in which he pursues this quest is through the use of strong figurative expressions and juxtaposition of alternate conditions.

The title of the poem, "Situation Report", is crucial to our understanding of it. It is a testimony of what obtains at present in the poet's society. Ngugi wa Thiong'o had asserted that:

> A writer's work "reflects one or more aspects of the intense economy, political, cultural and ideological struggles in a society. What he or she cannot do is to remain neutral. Every writer is a writer in politics. (*Writers* XVI)

Enekwe's poem opens with the simile of poverty flowing "like poison/ in the blood vessels of toiling people"(25). The masses who are the "toiling people" are not rewarded despite their sweat and sacrifice. Instead, scarcity and lack are the fruits of their toil.

Enekwe paints a vivid picture of Nigeria where social equality remains a far-away dream. He writes in the light of Emmanuel Obiechina's categorization of writers who operate "within the modern world order of human concern, benevolence, compassion and respect for human and individual rights" (2) and who use their media "to attack those negative values that undermine the sense of fullness of life and the realisation of man's potentials" (2).

Thus, for Nigerians, in the midst of social degeneration and want, "Fear knocks perpetually on their bones" (25). Fear, personified, emphasizes their collective penury and want; it is followed by the pessimism of "Dawn yields no sunshine" (25). Moreover the "ignorant, undernourished poor /blame fate for their misery" (25). But is it really fate or the selfishness of the powers that be? That is why the persona calls them "ignorant" because they are unaware of the misdeeds of those in power. To obtain favours from the rich the poor eulogise them "...and delude themselves/ that they too will flourish" (25). Because of their ability to rip off the poor there are "Yellow feelings where injustice reigns" (25).Yellow in this poem symbolizes aborted dreams and aggravates our awareness of the injustices meted out on the poem. The repetition "Yellow life of the poor/ yellow light at dusk when drunken bones/ shrivel" (25) outlines his humanist perception of the state of the poor.

The colour yellow is also connected with underdevelopment, marginal existence and stagnation. The poet's disgust is seen in the third stanza where he vividly portrays the lack of basic necessities for those who live on "potholes, muddy ponds and battered /pavement" (25). His concern about the dilapidated situation of the roads and homes of the poor is evident in the relationship between the poor, nature and elements.

Using fauna imagery, the persona decries the "rivers of crocodiles/ that bare their maws at the laughing/ whiteness of the sky/ the lonely, abandoned wretches trudge on" (25). The disillusionment and anger of the people are conveyed in their "deeding and dying, eyes blurred by salty/ sweat/ hearts burning with inchoate rage" (25). This poem conveys acute grief but ends on an optimistic note in the fourth and fifth stanzas. Change will come through "knowledge, intellection and work" (26); they will dislodge the powers of the rich and reject their manoeuvres. The rage will be directed by the firmness and potency of rockets and bazookas. The use of armoury is to emphasize that the downtrodden have refused to be underdogs and are ready to take the fight against the illusion of the "assumed permanence of injustice" (26). This situation of a privileged few growing richer and richer while the masses whose labour made them rich suffer in abject lack is a contemporary social reality in Africa. Thus African poets are preoccupied with adapting what Nelson Fashina terms "Marxist struggle against the agents of neo-colonialism and capitalism" (qtd. in Dasylva & Jegede 134). How will they create the kind of world they hope to achieve? "Through love for truth and beauty" they will "create that world/ where the hawk and the eagle can perch/ none displacing the other" (26). Osundare further underscores that Enekwe's call is "a call to quest, a pilgrimage; a call to arms, to peace" (vii).

Enekwe's ideological commitment should therefore be seen in his conviction that social change could come by massive awareness and willingness to fight corruption and political decadence. Shadrack Ambanasom, in "Pedagogy of the Deprived", defines the role of an artist as the "education of the masses especially the oppressed masses in such a way that they become imbued with a heightened sense of critical consciousness" (242). The last stanza reflects Enekwe's utopian longing for belonging, harmony and for a society where everyone can live at peace with another.

The poem "Beggars" is another case of how the masses suffer in the country. Enekwe address the new dispensation characterized by feelings of despair and frustration. It is sad that African leaders are worse than the colonial masters. "Beggars" provide vivid illustrations of the unimaginable distribution of wealth in a society where the citizens are emasculated and have to beg for survival. Thus the title becomes an extended metaphor for the marginalized and starved masses in postcolonial African societies. The corrupt, oppressive and dictatorial leaders amass all the wealth while the population suffer in abject poverty.

Enekwe wishes to share the experience of postcolonial African society on the throes of exploitation, embezzlement and poverty. He reinforces his arguments against the marginalization of the poor. The beggars are "hollow bowels" with their "beggars' bowls" who the politically affluent see "on our way/ everyday" (30). These particular lines are repeated in three stanzas of the five stanza poem. The repetition projects the precarious dilemma of the beggars in order to shock our sensitivity. Independence has not brought the necessary change in postcolonial Nigerian society. Chinua Achebe captures this in *Morning Yet on Creation Day* when he notes that

> Within six years of independence Nigeria was a cesspool of corruption and misrule. Public servants helped themselves freely of the nation's wealth... The politicians themselves were manipulated and corrupted by foreign business interests. (82)

In this unequal distribution of wealth, the poor gets poorer while the affluent get richer. Yet the state is supposedly a democracy. The synecdoche of "infant bellies" refer to the young beggars who have "tender bowels/ laden with slime" (30). The picture is grim. The beggars are incapable of enjoying life to the full: "Bleeding eyes/scare our souls/flood the shoals/ of the place of death" (30). The masses are disenchanted as the life for which they had wished eludes them. "Bleeding eyes" is a synecdoche for the beggars who scare the souls of those who pity their plight. The bleeding eyes that scare our souls emphasize the demeaning and hopeless condition of the people. We read the poem and we are left with a sad feeling of man's inhumanity to man.

In "Mammon Worship" the poet uses the dramatic device of exposition at the beginning of the poem to evoke an exploited society and introduce the themes of embezzlement and corruption. "They fence them with iron and concrete/ those palaces of granite/ built with blood money.../ monuments of sin in stone!" (8). The rest of the themes develop from the first part of the poem. This device is appropriate because it helps to bring out the preoccupation of the thematic poet with the lasciviousness and opulence of the rich. "Them" is the collective for the rich men's houses "built with blood money..." Thus the houses are "monuments of sin in stone!" because their hands are soiled with evil, they need "red-eyed security dogs / (to) walk around them/ to scare off nemesis" (8). What they are scaring off is retribution for their evil deeds.

Enekwe uses poetry as cogent means of rousing our consciousness and creating awareness of the ills of society. His commitment to socio-political and economic reconstruction of his society is evident in his persona's angst with power and exploitation politics of Africa. In using this poem to demonstrate the wilful emptying of the treasury by our leaders, Enekwe espouses the traditional belief that these rogues may have evaded guilt but they could not avoid the natural law of retribution.

The extravagance of the rich even during funerals is highlighted with the statement that "Funerals of rich rogues/ are for heavy feasting. Beer and champagne are aplenty/ for oily throats and sticky fingers" (8). We find ourselves in a world that is both familiar in postcolonial societies. They embezzle money and build rich homes and their funeral and wedding ceremonies are means of displaying their ill-gotten wealth. Their security dogs "chat with chicken bones" which the poor cannot afford (8). Enekwe's poetic method responds to the vicious Nigerian situation and exposes the corruptions of power and their consequences on the poor. Kathleen Greenfield in her essay "Murdering the Sleeps of Dictators: Corruption, Betrayal and the call to Revolution" in *The World of Ngugi* corroborates the argument that

> ...pens should be used to increase the anxiety of all oppressive regimes. At the very least the pen should be used to murder their crimes against the people and making them know that they are being seen. The pen may not always be mightier than the sword, but used in the service of truth, it can be a mighty force. (27)

The changing dynamics of power and identity in the postcolonial context is emphasized in the poem "Big Fish Eat Small Fish", "Dictatorship" and "What do you do with all your Power". Enekwe fashions the poem "Big Fish Eat Small Fish" from the need to expose the rich. The poor civilians ("small fish") are casualties of the big fish. The first line of this poem provides an answer as to whom the speaker is addressing. In the second line he explains "big men, small men/ in the belly of the night" (35). These lines are repeated in stanzas one, three and five for emphasis. There is an implied comparison where the "big fish" is the rich and the "small fish" is the poor. The world they inhabit in post-colonial society is far from idyllic. There is disillusionment caused by injustice, victimisation and oppression. The small fish is a symbol of man bereft of essence.

In the second stanza he reveals the true reason of his anger – the gross exploitation of the marginalized. Hence he laments how "king-sized fishes suck up the salt of the sea" (35). The metaphor of "king-sized fishes" stand for the rich rogues and affluent in the society who oppress the masses and place them in a position of otherness, socially, politically and economically. That explains why the "tiny ones lie prostrate" (35). Enekwe displays the disparity between the rulers and the ruled, the "Haves" and the "Have-nots". This is also intensified by the excessive exploitation of the masses by their leaders. The Nigerian critic, Amuta, says:

Since independence, the relationship between the post-colonial rulers and their subjects is characterised by a frightening disparity between the scandalous affluences of a few and the abject penury of the majority; a total neglect of public infrastructure and a near breakdown of all recognisable codes of ethical conducts. This situation has initiated a literature that is largely preoccupied with objectifying this reality with an underlying revolutionary aspiration. (58)

We may also infer from Enekwe's poem where "contractor-leaders carouse with lovers" (35) that the country's money is used by the leaders to pay for their night-outs and orgies hence our "drunken giants snore in granite towers". The metaphor of giants highlights the extent to which the leaders abuse the poor and exploit the nation. The harsh realities of life among the poor are also depicted in "Hungry workers, shrivelling into their pants" and who "scratch the dust like ants" (35). They work yet they are hungry. It means there is no recompense for their labour and service. This is a pointer to the fact that all times in society the rich amass wealth by refusing to pay for the labour given by the "small fish". The simile draws out their intense labour which is compared to the way ants laboriously scratch the ground. He addresses the continuous subjection of the poor where some have become scavengers to survive: "At the rising of the sun/ the poor escape their hovel" to "tear through refuse cans" to get food for the day. There is general disillusionment. Independence has proved a traumatic experience.

As depicted in the poem "Dictatorship", neo-colonial leadership is one of extortion, exploitation and assault on citizens who become casualties in their hands. Osundare notes that the poem "captures one of Africa's running political sores" (vi). As a social protest that censures politicians who indulge in swindling the country through stolen and inflated contracts, what strikes us first is the opening line:

"A gross beast /hauls itself across the sky" (9). The metaphor of the beast captures the ominous legacy the affluent leaders leave in their wake. They cast "a heavy night over the land/crushing the spirits in sunflowers /polluting the air with its stench /of rotten tongues between molars" (9).

Africa's dictators have been vicious and cold-blooded toward the opposition. The poet shocks the reader with this vivid language of rot and decay. Obviously, the poet wants us to capture the fiendish ingenuity of the oppressors invoked through the synecdoche of "rotten tongues" to showcase the effect of their monstrosity on society as emphasized in the second stanza where the persona laments: "A mist of despair/hangs over the blood-stained lake" (9). Mass despondency is "The mourning in this wind (which) wafts the ashes of the dead "(9). The idea of "mourning wind" calls attention to the sadness that surrounds the traumatised casualties of dictatorial regimes in Africa. Consequently their confused children bewail the injustice meted out to their parents in their "bewildered cries ...sunset-bound/ without homes" (9). The violence perpetuated in the society portrays the realities of the past and present as this dictatorship precipitates the disintegration of the Nigerian (African) society.

The rhetorical title of the poem "What do You Do With All Your Power?" piques our curiosity because it suggests an incongruous use of power and a disappointment in the rule of the elected: "What do you do/ with all your powers/ Oh Emperor,/ dizzy in your bower?"(33). As Osundare notes, "prominent throughout this collection is Enekwe's denunciation of excess, his constant recourse to moderation"(vi). The poet himself has placed it in parentheses that the poem is "For Dictators". The "Emperors" (Dictators) are dizzy because they are drunk with power and cannot control themselves. Christopher O'Reilly writes that "in some countries corruption has come to characterize much post independent politics" (6). Enekwe critiques this continuous misappropriation of the nation's coffers: "What joy do you get/ from stolen wealth,/ snatched jewels/ and seduced belles?"(33). He personalizes his disappointment in the sexual immorality that the likes of the Emperor indulge: "what do you do/ at dawn when it rains?"

This rhetorical question reveals the indecent nature of the rulers who plunder the nation's coffers to satisfy their sexual desire. That is why in the next line the persona reveals his disgust: "Tickle the nipples/ of tipsy ladies? Spray your anus/ with *eau de cologne*" (33). Next he introduces the fate that awaits them in the long run: "As you gloat over /murdered prophets /do you worry /about harvest time/ when the sun will darken /and grow cold?"(33-34).

CONCLUSION

Marching to Kilimanjaro is radical in the criticism of social malpractices and vices which undermine the well-being of the masses and consequently hinder the development of the nation. As a social commentator, Enekwe through the selected poems, represents facets of our social malaise in the themes of injustice, exploitation, suffering and corruption. He lives in a country which continues to remind him of that guilt as he struggles to understand the history of his own people. "Situation Report", "Beggars", "Mammon Worship", "Big Fish Eat Small Fish", "Dictatorship" and "What do you do with all your Power" are written with intensity and concentration of feeling.

The themes of poverty, hunger, injustice and embezzlement reveal the modern conditions of Nigerians which parallel that of many African countries where independence had propelled a new set of masters who mistreat their kith. Thus, Enekwe by portraying the ills of his society in his poetry, writes what is most important in a given moment of social and political history.

WORKS CITED

Achebe, Chinua. *Morning Yet On Creation Day*. London: Heinemann, 1979.

Ambanasom, S. A. "Pedagogy of the Deprived: A Study of the Plays of Victor Epie Ngome, Bole Butake and Bate Besong." *Epasa Moto*. Limbe: Pbook, 1996. 218-227.

---. *Education of the Deprived.* Yaoundé: Yaoundé Publishing, 2003.

Amuta, Chidi. *The Theory of African Literature*. London: Zed Books, 1989.

Dasylva, Ademola. O. and Oluwatoyin B. Jegede. *Studies in Poetry*. Ibadan: Stirlen-Horden Publishers, 2005.

Greenfield Kathleen. "Murdering the Sleeps of Dictators, Corruption, Betrayal and the call to Revolution." *The World of Ngugi wa Thiong'o*. Ed. Charles Cantalupo. New Jersey: Africa World Press, 1993: 27-42.

Meyer, Michael. *The Compact Bedford Introduction to Literature. Sixth Edition*. Boston: Bedford/St Martin's, 2003.

Murfin, Ross and Supryia. *The Bedford Glossary of Critical and Literary Terms*. New York: Bedford Books, 1997.

O'Reilly, Christopher. *Post-colonial Literature*. Cambridge: Cambridge UP, 2001.

Obiechina, Emmanuel. "The Writer and his Continent in Contemporary Nigerian Society." *Okike: An African Journal of New Writing*, 1998: 3-8.

Osundare Niyi. "Foreword." *Marching To Kilimanjaro*. Ossie Enekwe,

Enugu: Afa Press, 2005.

Wa Thiong'o, Ngugi. *Writers in Politics*. London: Heinemann, 1982.

10

Hope and Despair
IN ENEKWE'S *COME THUNDER*
Sunny Awhefeada

MODERN Nigerian literature has derived so much impetus from the nation's historical predicament. Ever since the emergence of Nigeria as a sovereign entity in 1960, the nation's literary representation has approximated its growth in terms of keeping pace with its chequered trajectory. The Nigerian Civil War which raged from 1967-1970 is one dark index of the nation's history and has been the subject of a great deal of Nigerian literature. The war, beyond providing material for literature, marked a turning point in the career of several Nigerian writers as much as it begot a new generation of writers whose apprehension of the Nigerian condition departs radically from that of the writers of the pre-Civil War era.

The turning point in the career of the pre-Civil War writers manifests in the jolt provided by the cataclysmic events of the war. This jolting engendered an urgent necessity for the writers to focus on the burning issues of the day, which at that time was the Civil War. Bamikunle writes that "each work of art finds inspiration in the historical social realities in which the author finds himself" (73). The war and the tragic events it engendered were too compelling for the writers to ignore and continue their hitherto preoccupation with the past which Chinua Achebe eloquently advocated in the telling words that "the past needs to be recreated not only for the enlightenment of our detractors, but even for our own education" (157). However, imperative as this assertion might have been, the reality of a horrendous war did not allow the writers to ruminate on the past and recreate it. Writers, whether Wole Soyinka, Chinua Achebe, J.P. Clark, or Christopher Okigbo, found urgent themes in the events of the war. The end of the war also threw up a new generation of writers who not only wrote about it, but also engaged post-war Nigerian socio-economic and political reality. Some of these new writers witnessed the war first hand, while others heard from a distance its blood-chilling echoes. Amongst these post-war writers are Ossie Enekwe, Pol Ndu, Isidore Okpewho, Obiora Udechukwu, I.N.C. Aniebo, Andrew Ekwuru, Ken Saro-Wiwa, Festus Iyayi, Niyi Osundare, Kole Omotoso, Femi Osofisan, Tanure Ojaide, Eddie Iroh, etc. These writers recreated the horrors of war in poetry, prose and drama. The chain of writings on the Nigerian civil war is unending. Amuta comments:

> In the growing body of Nigerian national literature, works, directly based on or indirectly deriving from the war experience constitute the largest number of literary products on any single aspect of Nigerian history to date. (85)

The civil war has yielded and continues to yield more literary harvest. This view is also reinforced by Oladitan when he says: "one is immediately struck by the quality of production and the variety of approach to what is essentially the same subject matter" (10). In 2006, thirty-six years after its cessation, the war played into literary relevance once more as it became the subject-matter of Adichie's novel *Half of Yellow Sun*.

Ossie Onuora Enekwe is one of those Nigerian writers who came to literary prominence on the blazing wings of the Civil War. However, significant as his creative ouvre is, he remains in the league of those neglected writers whose names prop up occasionally in literary discourses. Most of Enekwe's writings dwell on the gory and cataclysmic episodes of the war and the reaction of human beings especially the Igbo on whose soil the grueling war took place. One striking feature of Nigerian civil war literature is the preponderance of writers of Igbo extraction of which Enekwe is one.

Enekwe's writings illuminate battle scenes, portraying the soldiers who do battle, the effect of war on the civilian populace, its cruelty, tragedy, loss and other numerous vistas of armed conflict. These thematic inclinations are privileged in *Broken Pots*, a collection of poems, and very significantly in *Come Thunder*, a novel, which is the focus of this discourse.

The novel *Come Thunder* derives its title from one of Christopher Okigbo's war poems also of the same caption. The most relevant lines in the poem appropriated by Enekwe reads:

> Now that the triumphant march has entered the last
> Street corners,
> remember, O dancers, the thunder among the cloud.
> (*Labyrinths* 66)

The metaphor of thunder foregrounds the calamitous war. The devastation, especially of human lives, caused by the war, was pervasive, and this has been expressed in J.P. Clark's threnodic poem "Casualties". Enekwe's *Come Thunder* recreates vivid battle scenes as the soldiers fight and die in a gory war. The reader is taken through gun duels by the child-soldier, Meka Chinedu, around whom the events revolve. The novel straddles between the opposites of hope and despair which provide this chapter's title. In the novel's early pages the reader encounters a populace, the Balans and their soldiers full of zest and hope that victory was going to be theirs. They are propelled by a self-righteous quest for vengeance over the massacre of their people by Zagians. However, as the war progresses the Balans starved of ammunition suffer heavy losses and their hope degenerates into despair. This mood is captured by the narrator as follows: "Hope and despair in combat in the mind. Let the rebels give up... before it is too late" (109). The unexpected turn of the events of the war justifies Paine's notion that "war involves in its progress a chain of unforeseen and unsupposed circumstances that no human wisdom can calculate its ends".

The story begins with Meka "who had run away from home to join the Balan Army. A puny little boy, his ribs were discernible" (1). The boy Meka is propelled by a strong patriotic desire to defend his homeland against an invading army. Indeed, this patriotism pervades all of Bala. At the recruitment centre, Enekwe's descriptive power tells the reader about "thousand of young men who are eager to join the army" and "most of all these people had come from the farthest towns and villages in Bala" (1). The patriotic zeal demonstrated by the Balans is complimented by their readiness for self-preservation through fighting. Hear the people's voice:

> "God is with us... We can't wait for the vandals to kill us off before we realized what their intentions are," someone said, "only a tree hears that it will be cut down and stays put." (12)

Thus the Balan fighting spirit is sustained by the zest which usually accompanies determination for self-preservation. For them, to fight is to survive. This view is enunciated by Meka when he tells his sisters: "We are better soldiers. If we continue killing them, they will be forced to stop fighting" (31). The "them" in Meka's utterance refers to the vandals in the quotation preceding this. Running through the narrative embedded in *Come Thunder* are streaks of provocation, vengeance and resistance. The narrator says:

> Meka was transformed into a warrior when he saw refugees numerous as locusts returning from the north. At the Asa railway station, he saw them – a faded mass, wrapped in broad, blood-soaked bandages.
> Many were without legs, eyes or ears. (2)

The Balans feel, and justifiably so, a sense of being annihilated through a well programmed pogrom. This as the novel unfolds provides the *casus belli* for the war. Even Meka's comrade at arms, the young Amobi, joins the Army because as he says: "They killed my father and nearly killed me. It was God who saved my life" (7). He goes on to say: "My father won't die like that, like a dog…even if they kill me, I don't care, but I must kill them…"(16). The quest for vengeance becomes a motivating factor for those who enlist in the Army.

However, not every body shares in the provocation and quest for vengeance which spur Meka and others. Meka's parents, Mr. and Mrs. Chinedu, did not get enveloped by the mood of war. Their attitude is that of restraint, caution and disinterestedness which almost disillusions Meka. According to the narrator, Meka's mother "believed that soldering was a dangerous game. A soldier in uniform was like a flower just before the Harmattan" (2). This attitude dominates Meka's parents' psychology throughout the novel. He never gets their blessing to fight in the war. His sisters plead with him to leave the army, but he refuses. This throws his family into a silent domestic crisis. His father degenerates into a psychological wreck just as his mother has cause to lament and cry again and again. The gloom in Meka's home is replicated in many other homes and it gives an insight into how the war affects families negatively. Meka having been estranged from his family, and undergone the rigours of military training, gets transformed from the puny little boy that he was into a tested soldier ready to fight in the trenches. From this moment the reader is taken through different battle scenes and the tragedies they wrought. At the war front the reader encounters soldiers that are almost eaten up by the anxiety, fear and the eventuality of death. Meka's first encounter with the enemies goes thus:

> From about two hundred yards right in their front the enemy emerged singing:
> *O-shebe yeah*
> *O-shebe. Yea*
> Meka gazed at them. They hardly looked like enemies. The whole scene was like a game in school, a kind of:
> Kangoro,
> Oh Kangoro
> Catch me if you can.
> Oh catch me if you can.
> Meka wondered about his carbine. Suppose I fire and nothing comes off. Firing at fellow human beings ...There were about fifteen of the enemy advancing, moving as if they were going for a hunt... Umana shouted, "Fire"
> The response was deafening. Volleys of bullet poured on the advancing troops and almost all of them went down. (41)

This episode recounts Meka's initiation into real battle. Before the shooting ordered by his commander, Umana, Meka and the other soldiers had dug trenches and nervously awaited the advance of the enemy. The commander himself "was becoming afraid....Nothing could beat the Zagian fire power" (36). But the fear does not deter the soldiers from fighting. They hope to spring a surprise on the enemy, and this they do. However the enemy does not give up. They re-organize and attack as portrayed in the following excerpt:

> "They don flank us," shouted the sergeant, dashing for cover...
> Zagain bullets whirred and clapped over their hands. Meka heard their yells and his blood congealed inside him. The Zagian troops advanced and kept their bullets flying...Meka had never seen anything like that before, even in the movies. He felt like digging into the entrails of earth for refuge, since no matter how he rolled or placed his head, the enemy bullets seemed to be searching for him. (41-42)

At the end of this fatal exchange of gun fire many of the soldiers on both sides became casualties, and a harvest of death followed. For the first time Meka comes close to a corpse and even assisted in burying the dead soldiers. The commander sees him shading tears and consoles him.

Many more battles are portrayed in *Come Thunder,* and Enekwe's descriptive power and manipulation of visual and acoustic imagery make it appear as if the reader were watching a war movie. In another scene where the Balans raid the Zagian camp, the narrator presents the incident as follows:

> The Machine gunner pressed the trigger. Like chunks of flames, bullets began to stream towards the doors and windows of the camp. The sounds of the machine gun shattered the air and shook the ground on which they were laying... its sound was like that of a motorcycle that had cast off its rider while its engine kept beating. The very rhythm of the machine gun fire troubled even the fire in

the deep recesses of his belly. It was sound of death in the dawn. (780)

The events in the foregoing scene could evoke only fear and terror in the soldiers, the killer and the killed. However, the soldiers do not give up, at least not just yet. They keep on fighting and the war in all its destructiveness rages on claiming lives. As the battles multiply in their monstrosity the Balan soldiers are goaded on by the goodwill and support of the civilian population. One such example of civilian goodwill and support for the soldiers is played out when Meka offers to pay for riding in a taxi. The driver reduces the fare because Meka is a soldier; the driver says:

> "Na three shillings, we day charge for this place. But, I go take one shilling from you, because, as long as you people de fight well we go treat you well. Because this na people's war. (33)

Such encouragement and show of goodwill would be the tonic to spur the Balam soldiers on. There are other instances of support for the fighting soldiers. For example a wealthy chief volunteers to provide food for the troops while the Asa women tirelessly do the cooking. The Red Cross girls also volunteer their services to the cause of the war.

But goodwill alone does not win a war. The Balans are starved of ammunition, while the Zagian soldiers that are well armed continue to win one battle after another. The truth of the hapless situation of the Balan Army is summed up by one of the commanders thus while addressing the solders: "No doubt you have seen that the enemy has more and better equipment that we have. Nevertheless, we must win this war; we have no choice" (74). So with such words the soldiers are goaded on to continue fighting even as they are being wiped out by

Zagian soldiers.

The story reaches its climax with the death of Meka's commander, Umana, who can be described as an efficient Balan officer winning several battles despite the odds stacked against his troops. Umana's last battle before his death depicts him as a gallant soldier who risks, but becomes a casualty of the war. The narrator creates the scenario of Umana's death as follows:

> Umana was hit in the chest near the heart and when the two privates rushed forward to carry him, they were caught down. They died immediately, while Umana groaned and twisted in the dust...
> When Meka saw blood dripping from Umana's chest, his head went in a whirl, and his heart fainted; however, placing his arm on Umana's chest he tried to stop the blood, but it flowed on, passing between his finger...the sergeant said, "our officer don die-o". (84)

The death of Umana, like those of others who died in the war, highlights the tragic dimension of the conflict. That such a fine officer like Umana as well as hordes of soldiers perished in the war foregrounds the cruelty of it and the wastage of humanity. Throughout the narrative, the soldiers as well as the civilians live in perpetual fear of death.

Umana's death marks the turning point of the narrative. Morale drops among the soldiers in the war front just as the hitherto supportive civilian population start to vilify the Balan troops as they lose series of battles. The soldiers also rebel against some of their officers for sabotaging the war effort and even kill them in the process. The civilians also hunt down the soldiers especially the ones fleeing from the deadly battle front.

However, beyond the deaths, loss, psychological wreckage and overarching gale of tragedy narrated in *Come Thunder*, there are other streaks that deserve commentary loudly or faintly in the novel.

The narrator punctuates the yarn with an undertone of ambivalence. This ambivalence accounts for Meka's parents' withdrawal of support for him when he joins the army. The narrative note of ambivalence is further given accent by the officers when one of them says the following about Major Ndu, a principal actor in the war:

> But I don't really know his attitude to this war. I watched him when Bala declared independence. Others were relieved and happy, but Ndu seemed to be in great pain, his face as cold and stolid as rock. (60)

A critical consideration of the effusions of Balans might lead to the question: "were the Balans not misguided by selfish leaders who wanted to be rulers of their own country?" "Where the Balans in the know of the real issues that culminated in the war?" "Did they act on emotion rather than reason?" In the cause of the story a faint but critical and introspective voice is heard in the following dialogue:

> "But, it's our people who first started it," the man whose car was abandoned said.
> "How?"
> "You remembered the new year coup...." (96)

The conversation, muffled as it is, when placed in its historical context will condition the reader's appreciation of the war and its artistic recreation. Some of the participants in the factual events that metamorphosed into the fiction of *Come Thunder* have documented the unfortunate events that snowballed into full scale war. Ademoyega's *Why We Struck,* Madiebo's *The Nigerian Revolution and the Biafran War,* among other chronicles of that epoch, situated the civil war as a corollary of the 15 January, 1966 coup during which

168

mostly Northern leaders and soldiers were killed. S.G. Ikoku saw the war as the final consequence of the events started by the coup that was predominately staged by Igbo officers.

Come Thunder, however, is not all about fear, death and gloom. There are a few instances of the other side of life. There are occasional banters and humour. The officers, once in a while, indulge in carnality and easy life, lusting after women, loving and even getting married. The commander, Umana falls in love with Ada and marries her during the war. At his death, Ada is heavily pregnant with a child that will continue with his lineage. This justifies his indulging in love even in the war.

Enekwe's narrative is vivid and brings the battle scenes first hand to the reader. His ability to gauge and recreate the human mood helps in navigating the people's psychology and their attitudes towards the soldiers in the beginning and the despair which enshrouded the Balans in the end. The novel portrays a heroic people that are led to war in a most helpless condition. Their heroism is further adumbrated by the valiant effort and sacrifices they make at running the war, however, futile. It can be read as a tribute to the soldiers who fight and died for the cause they believed in.

Works Cited

Achebe, C. "The Role of the Writer in a New Nation." *Nigeria Magazine*. No. 8. June 1964.

Ademoyega, A. *Why We Struck*. Ibadan: Evans Brothers, 1981.

Adichie, C. *Half of a Yellow Sun*. Lagos: Farafina, 2006.

Amuta, C. "Literature of the Nigerian Civil War." *Perspectives on Nigerian Literature: 1700 to the present*. Vol. 1. Ed. Y. Ogunbiyi, Lagos: Guardian

Books, 1988.

Bamikunle, A. "Literature as Historical Process: A Case Study of Ojaide's *Labyrinths of the Delta*." *African Literature and African Historical Experience*. Ed. Chidi Ikonne, Ibadan: Heinemann, 1991.

Enekwe, O. O. *Broken Pots*. Nsukka: Afa Press, 1977.

———. *Come Thunder*, Enugu: Fourth Dimension, 1984.

Ikoku, S.G. "Nigeria Comes of Age." *Africa Now*. October, 1981.

Madiebo, A. *The Nigerian Revolution and the Biafran War*. Enugu: Fourth Dimension, 1980.

Nnolim, C. "Trends in the Nigerian Novel." *Literature and National Consciousness*. Ed. Ernest Emenyonu. Ibadan: Heinemann, 1989.

Okigbo, C. *Labyrinths*. Ibadan: Heinemann, 1986.

Oladitan, O. "The Nigerian Crisis in the Nigerian Novel." *New West African Literature*. Ed. K. Ogungbesan. London: Heinemann, 1977.

 Reviews

11

A Sacred Endeavour

Book: *Marching to Kilimanjaro* pp ix + 63
Author: Onuora Ossie Enekwe
Publisher: Afa Press, Enugu
ISBN   978-30033-2-1 (paperback)
Reviewer: GMT Emezue

COMPRISING forty poems, Enekwe's *Marching to Kilimanjaro* is thematically grouped in three sections: "Titillation and Pain", "Situation Report" and "The Lion Wakes". The award winning Nigerian poet Niyi Osundare in the "Foreword" points at the contrast of views adopted by the poet which makes the collection "not a mere annotation of African topography" but a perception of "contrasts (that) extend to... man-woman, Europe-Africa, city-village" (i). Through this perception of opposites, Enekwe's poetry is laden with references to a volatile modern Africa where Western democracy is synonymous with evil, oppression, exploitation of natural resources, and disenfranchisement. The liberation struggles in Southern Africa and dictatorship in Central Africa – Zaire and Congo – are significant concerns to the poet-artiste.

One may not be too eager to agree that in this volume Enekwe cuts the figure of that "Okigboesque prodigal in search of roots, so eager to find that primordial cord in the navel of the earth" (Osundare iii) since for Enekwe's realism, and for one who agrees literature is political art[1], the African issue within the larger realities went beyond the mystical urgency that was Okigbo's prodigal quest. Thus reaching to the peaks of Kilimanjaro assumes the means to overcome limitations inherent in the abject lack of true freedom and liberty in the homeland. Expressed from the affirmative grounding in roots that has been the hallmark of his poetry since *Broken Pots*, Enekwe's new collection engages the reader in a further interrogation of the constructs and negations of an African dream.

The first part "Titillation and Pain" sets off this epic mission in the incantatory stage of the quest as offered by the beginning "Agbogho Mmonwu" poem. This section will take us through phases of decadence and corruption in many parts of the African continent. It is presaged by adopting a tone of supplication and invoking the kinship of mutual love for art, creativity and melody between poet and "Agbogho (maiden) Mmonwu (spirit)" who is addressed thus:

> Teach me to fly
> Fleet
> Wriggle
> And make miracle figures in space. (3)

This traditional opening employed by the African artiste has proven an important formulaic device for few contemporary Nigerian poets of sound critical awareness. It is a way of connecting, not only the written (modern) with the oral (traditional), but also the spiritual and the mundane. The purpose must be found in the African perception of art as a stirring of spiritual energies which impel the artist towards the removal of any destructive disequilibrium in the human condition, and for a return "to order and cosmic health". Thus as Zulu Sofola rightly reveals,

> in the vision of the artist, ... heroic characters emerge who confront bravely the problem and through them the spectator reflects on self and the state of cosmic ill health in his society, and moves to re-order himself and his community. Hence art is defined among Africans ... as a medium through which a sick and battered humanity may be healed and restored to life. (7)

As art is such a sacred endeavour in Africa, then it is not uncommon for true poet-artistes to begin their performance with incantations and such other traditional formulae through which they establish the sanctity of their role. Enekwe's overture is reminiscent of Udechukwu's "mad man" who proclaims his psychic invincibility at the beginning of his poetry:

> TRUTH is Iron
> is my A.D.C
>
> Maggots or worms cannot touch me.
> ...
> I am frog
> Jumping cannot kill me.
> I am wind:
> Can I succumb to a snare? (39)

It is also similar to Ce's poet-persona in "A Farewell to the old ways" who, in an "unanchored reference to graffiti" (Hamilton 99), avows his calling to tread "lonely high long ways" and "thick forests" gaining illumination with the break of "the shining light of soul" to follow "the other route" of alternate voice of the people (9). Enekwe, by using the phrase "teach me," locates his own "dialogue" in the region of respectful familiarity, where both minds participate in a mutual "giving and taking" which is rather unlike the grovelling acolyte of Okigbo's "Mother Idoto."

From the above perspective it is easy to imagine why Enekwe cautiously begins with this incantatory opening "Agbogho Mmonwu" in order to draw his reader-audience into the sacred act of performance (reading) which this collection appropriates. This way political or personal issues addressed in the poems are collectively raised from "mundane" to semi-religious dimensions. "Mother" which is the poem that follows, nudges at the hope of fulfillment through the woman who "…loosens her bra/and bares her bosom" to nurture and nourish a hungry baby. The allusion of feminine warmth does not only stop at male/female, mother/child relationships but also becomes a metaphor for self actualisation in the epic quest of reaching the heights of Kilimanjaro. If brought to bear on the decadent condition of African leadership, this might hint at the possibility of a future hope.

Other poems like "The Sweet Things", "Lagos," and "Mammon Worship" all reveal different faces of Africa's moral and social decadence. The poetic scenes move from the economic aridity of "the echo and snarl/of dry pockets…" ("Lagos" 5) through

> … broken mud
> gaping
> starved, breathless
> … with lines
> of age, pain and batter. (6)

of contaminated humanity to "Palaces of granite/built with blood money", and where

> corpulent mouths and anuses
> open and close the gates of hell. (8)

These are vivid images measuring the scale of political and moral decay prevalent in the African continent.

"Solitude" and "Raven Day" are dirges that reveal other aspects of African life. Like all things in nature people die at their appointed time and change is the only constant in human nature. The inevitability of death resounds in "Solitude", dedicated to the renowned Igbo critic, Nnabuenyi Ugonna, with Darwinian notions of social progression, and the existentialist futility of human endeavour. Our lives all become "voices of humanity trapped in mud", "memories of loved ones lost in the wind" (11) and also:

> ... pieces of cloud
> sailing gently to eternity. (11)

This is in spite of the beauty of nature with

> beautiful faces in a crowd
> honeyed voices in a passing encounter
> laughter and glitter
> of teenage girls
> (and) toddle of infants
> swaying dance of flowers... (10)

The sense of futility and nostalgia underscore the sorrow that wells up at the loss of our few great ones, and the recollection of all the beautiful things that must pass away. The mood of despair is carried into "Raven day," a poem dedicated to late Mamman Vatsa who was killed for an alleged coup by the military authorities of

Nigeria under General Babangida. Once again, the idea of fatalism is communicated through the imagery of

> Death (which) approaches with its basket
> For a harvest of skulls. (12)

The tragic injustice perceived in the death of General Vatsa is captured as

> ... misery of flowers
> rushed by fetid waters. (12)

Thus, while "Solitude" and "Raven day" relish a fatalistic acceptance of the unchangeable, the poem "Mandatory Song" seeks the *raison d'etre* for all the "Needles and Pains" that define human existence.

The section that Enekwe calls "Situation Report" is a panorama of the political landscape of Africa, a landscape mired in repression, political clientelism, and electoral malpractices in different parts of Africa. The politicians and military rulers indicted here are described as "King's 'Yes men'" (27), "Toads in a Pond" (28), "Emperor" (33), "Big fish," "malignant weeds", "king-sized fishes" (35) and "Beasts of the jungle" (40). Their actions impoverish the people who are

> The lonely abandoned wretches ...
> Breeding and dying, eyes blurred by salty
> Sweat,
> Hearts burning with inchoate rage. (25)

The arrangement of the poem in this section follows a "cause and effect" pattern. Poems dealing on the causes (like the actions of corrupt political gladiators) of the sterility, poverty and decadence in

Africa are closely followed or preceded by poems showing the travails of Africa's poor. References to womanhood, like in "Black woman" and "Prayer for peace", exploit classical tropes of caring mother and fatal woman to situate "the woman simultaneously in a symbol of destruction, nurture and enigma ("Black woman"). The plastered Mona Lisa smile of "...gentle, flowing sadness" (29) in the women of Africa addresses the stoicism of humanity in the face of problems and misfortunes.

The last section "The Lion Wakes" is a collation of ideas that resound with hope. Throughout the section, the reader is made witness to the coming hope with which the

> Cobras uncoil from withered branches
> And stand firm by the path (43) –

and

> ... the Lion wakes
> eyes, a flash of arrows
> over the plains. (45)

Here finally the day of Africa's liberty has come. We are enjoined to usher in "a moment of lightning and laughing thunder" (48) or "songs and bullets of.../ angry returning children" ("Zaire" 51). It is the dawn of "Uhuru". It is the "day, we take/ the hill called Freedom" (54). It is freedom not only from European /African confrontation but from the tyranny of the local collaborator when the

> ... blood River regales in the sun
> and washes its banks
> for the dance of tomorrow. (60)

It is also the day that the

> Chants of liberty will thrill us
> Across battered parapets
> And our loves will come to us at dawn
> Fresh with the perfume of roses. (62)

The poems in this section proclaim hopes of victory, and of survival, after the battle against political and economic slavery has been fought and won. Like his traditional counterpart, Enekwe ends his collection with a performance poem, "Aftermath", which has a "Chorus" to simulate audience participation. In line with the predominant message in this section, the "song" celebrates the hope of a beautiful future where

> There will grow again
> On the moldy scars of time
> Of the purple battleground. (63)

The day will no doubt come when

> Flowers will bloom again
> Green, lush and beautiful
> Despite sighing, mourning blades. (63)

This song of victory and joy aptly brings the collection to a climaxed ending. Enekwe, a true African artist, derives strength from this utilization of performance and song in poetry. Many poems here are realized through the narrative mode which has a persona or "voice" that speaks and expresses the ultimate vision for society. Copious descriptive epithets and images help to sustain the mood and highlight the hidden sentiments in expression. The "Black Woman", whose lips are "two petals pressed together", echoes Keats in his Autumnal ode to the "Season of mist and mellow fruitfulness...". For Enekwe, like Diop and Senghor before him, black womanhood is our own

>   Queen of perpetual smile
>   And gentle, flowing, sadness
>   ...
>   (whose) warm breasts
>   Light in the corridors of life. (29)

Irony (or sometimes, sarcasm) also appears as a dominant artistic weapon of confrontation, especially in the two sections where the poet reexamines the exploitation and dehumanization of African humanity. Although the lance is thrust at blacks who are instruments of this continental disorder, yet sometimes references draw to white-vs-black conflicts as the cause of the African problem in the twenty-first century.

Unlike his earlier collection of *Broken Pots* where a few poems deviate from the central Biafran war theme, all the poems in this collection devolve upon common ground: the overall performance of hope and affirmation of human survival against all odds. The cadence grafted upon the rhythm of words evokes benign aspirations, and despite the painful issues at stake in the first two sections, the voice achieves equilibrium of mood and tone.

In this collection Enekwe has used his craft as Sofola suggests: "to create a new vision for growth renewal, regeneration and edification of man for a wholesome life and a better community" (5). His celebration of some of Africa's heroes is not a mere exercise in the panegyric. It sustains the Afrocentric position that

> (in) the vision of the artist, particularly in the art of performance, heroic characters emerge who confront bravely, the problem and through them the spectator reflects on self and the state of cosmic ill-health in his society, and moves to reorder himself and his community. (7)

Thus Samora Machel, Nnabuenyi Ugonna, Mamman Vatsa, Oliver Tambo, Antonio Agostingho Neto, Robert Mugabe, Nelson Mandela, Julius Nyerere and Murtala Mohammed are icons whose examples may be emulated in Africa.

Of course art is universal as its perception of the world cuts across continental boundaries. Yet it begins from subjective perspectives from which it reaches out to the fringes of the universe. For Enekwe, this subjective front is the African landscape with its myriads of political differences and cultural complexities. Through Enekwe's poetry, instances of human greed, expressed through dictatorship and lust for power, become parameters for critiquing the folly of African leaders. And in carrying out this activity, Enekwe's *Marching to Kilimanjaro* attempts to "heal and restore the life of a sick and battered humanity" (8).

NOTE

[1] In a discourse with Enekwe on African literature first published in the *African Literary Journal,* B5 2005, the poet acknowledges his influences as

going beyond the tragic human waste of the civil war: "...when I travelled outside the country, I became more aware of what was happening. I became exposed to things going on around the world. I read other writers like Pablo Neruda, Ibsen etc. I also interacted with other writers like Amiri Baraka who was a close friend. So all these acted as sources of influence on my writings. For instance my other collection of poems *Marching to Kilimanjaro* reacts to other issues in Africa..." (p. 47)

WORKS CITED

Ce, Chin. "A Farewell." *An African Eclipse*. Enugu: Handel Books, 2000.

Enekwe, O. Onuora. *Marching to Kilimanjaro*. Nsukka: Afa Press, 2005.

Hamilton, G.A.R. "Beyond Subjectificatory Structures: Chin Ce 'In the season of another life.'" *The African Journal of New Poetry*. 1 V3, 2006 95-117.

Osundare, Niyi. "Foreword." *Marching to Kilimanjaro*. Onuora O. Enekwe, Nsukka: Afa Press, 2005.

Sofola, Zulu. *The Artist and the Tragedy of a Nation*. Ibadan: Caltop Publications, 1994.

Udechukwu, Obiora. "Affirmations." *What the Mad man Said*. Obiora Udechukwu, Bayreuth: Boomerang Press, 1990.

― ― ―. "What the Mad man Said." *What the Mad man Said*. Obiora Udechukwu, Bayreuth: Boomerang Press, 1990.

12

From Dream into Nightmare

Book: *Come Thunder*
Author: Onuora Ossie Enekwe
Publisher: Fourth Dimension
Reviewer: Chidi Okonkwo

COME Thunder is a story about war. It is also a story of growth: a boy's rite of passage through secure adolescence to perilous manhood. Above all, it is a study of the transformation of hope into despair, and dream into nightmare.

Set in the early months of the Nigerian-Biafran war (or Zaga-Bala war as Onuora Enekwe has it), the novel tells the story of Meka Chinedu, aged 15, who sneaked away from home and a caring family to enlist in the Bala army. His head fermenting with enthusiasm and patriotism, Meka also dreams of attaining the heroic stature of his pop-culture and cinema idols. The novel explores the brutal tearing away of successive layers of Meka's illusion against the background of the rapidly crumbling morale in Bala army and society.

Come Thunder differs in at least two respects from other novels which treat the Nigeria-Biafra war: first in Enekwe's choice of a teenage character as protagonist, and next in his exploring the subject matter beyond the physical thrills and terrors of war. Thrills and terrors there are aplenty, but these are severely subordinated to the psychological task of probing the mental and emotional processes of people caught in the whirls of incomprehensible and uncontrollable events.

When the novel opens, an all-pervading effervescence of hope, confidence, patriotic pride and sense of common destiny unites all Balans. Behind this solidarity lies a Masada-complex: memories of the recent pogrom unleashed upon Balans in the federation to which they had formerly belonged, and a grim determination that never again will Balans be slaughtered like animals as long as the Bala army holds its own against the better equipped and implacable enemy. It retains its morale and the people's support. Once reverses set in, however, the army's fighting spirit quickly collapses.

Enekwe reveals the process through a series of sharply etched incidents. In meticulous detail, he traces the oscillations of military fortune and popular mood. Meka's first shock comes with his discovery that as a soldier he is just another unit of force in the army's striking power. His perception of his voluntary enlistment as a "heroic and patriotic" act deserving of the nation's special gratitude is revealed as naïve. There is profound irony in Meka's resentful musing "... as if we were prisoners". For he is indeed a prisoner; a prisoner of his own naive, adolescent idealism and dreams of glory, and a prisoner of the great events.

Come Thunder is structured on ironies and contrasts. Alternating his narrative focus between Bala army barracks, battle fronts and rear positions (especially Meka's family), Enekwe effectively evokes the physical, moral and psychological ravages of war. Complementing this expository device is Enekwe's reiterative scheme: the use of variations upon a basic pattern of incidents to mark changing moods, changing perceptions of the war, changing responses to it, and the rapid degeneration into chaos. A proper war atmosphere is additionally evoked through dialogue, characters' reminiscences, close-up shots of actual battles, and inspired imagery which makes experience palpable and endows actions with multiple significance.

In the opening chapter of the novel, Meka quickly sheds his glamorized image of war as he discovers loneliness, hunger, fear, his own insignificance, and the sorry state of the army. But these discoveries also constitute a definite phase in his initiation into the mysteries of living and dying. The second chapter reveals the enormous goodwill the army enjoys among the citizenry. Taxi drivers give free rides to Meka and his friend Amobi, and itch to take up arms against the remorseless federal enemy. But while Amobi's mother is happy that her soldier son will soon avenge her husband's murder during the pogrom, Meka's parents feel resentful and betrayed by his joining the army. Then an enemy air raid shocks the civilian populace into some bitter recognition of Bala's military weakness. As enemy gains increase, repressed dissatisfaction and rebelliousness burst out. When rumours of persistent acts of treachery and sabotage begin to circulate like a foul odour, the slide into despair turns into a stampede. Military reverses also bring out the worst examples of callousness, avarice and sheer opportunism from the people. At the battlefronts, mutinous troops shoot their commanders and soldiers fleeing the battlefronts are arrested and humiliated by civil defense patrols.

For Meka and his platoon, the turning point comes with the death of their exemplary commander Lieutenant Umana. The death leaves the platoon thrashing about in bewilderment. Through it, Enekwe also makes a telling point about the transience of happiness. It robs Meka of the comfort and security he has briefly enjoyed as Lt Umana's batman. The Lieutenant himself had only just recently wed his Red Cross sweetheart. Enekwe's brief examination of the agony and dilemma of the officers who had to break the news to the widow, and the widow's own anguish, is one of the most memorable portions of the novel.

With 116 pages, *Come Thunder* is rather slight. It is, therefore, a sign of Ossie Onuora Enekwe's gifts and skills as a novelist that within the limited space he has been able to create a work that is rich in texture and multilayered in meaning. *Come Thunder* is a tightly woven and austere narrative which effortlessly takes the reader through successive depths of individual and corporate nightmare.

13

The Marks of Carnage

Book: *The Last Battle and Other Stories*
Author: Onuora Ossie Enekwe
Publisher: Minaj Publishers
Reviewer: Olayiwola Adeniji

THE Nigerian civil war marked an important phase in the evolution of a national literature for the country. As a result of the carnage, creative writers began to shift from an almost rabid concern for cultural nationalism to a deeper concern for regeneration of a society at the danger of self annihilation.

Almost three decades after the incestuous carnage the same questions are still being asked. Was the war necessary? And has the nation learnt any lessons from the self-inflicted tragedy? Quite unfortunately, the problems that led to the war are still there. So artists who Alexander Solzhenitsyn says function to convey people's irrefutable condensed experiences from generation to generation are left with no other choice but to remain in the business of social diagnoses, reminding the people "where the rain began to beat them" as Achebe had put it.

Onuora Ossie Enekwe's *The Last Battle and Other Stories* is the latest addition to what in the nation's literary patrimony is now referred to as "civil war literature". But this might be too quick a conclusion to make because a more careful reading will reveal that although the civil war forms the context of some of the stories, the collection performs a bigger function. Enekwe uses it as the origin of the recurring vicious cycle of pain, disillusionment, desperation and destruction that is continually unleashed on the national psyche by forces inimical to social growth. This is in consonance with the school of thought, which believes that literature must be an organic function of a nation's history.

The Last Battle and Other Stories contains ten short stories of varying lengths, which at various times, between 1973 and 1994, made appearances in both local and international journals and anthologies. In the civil war stories there is the prevailing evocation of anguish and the predatory tendencies in human nature as displayed by the various actors in the war. The physical and psychological impact on these characters creates in the reader a cathartic effect. Such collocations as "dull depressing morning; babies with sunken and swollen cheeks; etc all go to lay bare the hideous futility and horrors of the fratricidal war. Enekwe presents in each of the stories, a character that symbolizes the "anonymous millions of casualties" and their struggle to survive the ordeal of oppression and privation.

Even among the soldiers in the battle there is injustice and the title story, "The Last Battle", more than any other, reveals this unfortunate situation. Soldiers who have god-fathers enjoy special privileges while the unfortunate ones like Joseph Umeh are moved from one hot sector to another and, no matter their bravado and exploits, nobody recognizes them. Umeh has two bullets inside his buttocks which qualifies him for a transfer to the rear instead he, like most others, has to die "so that the mighty lords may live and enjoy", says the narrator. Captain Ofili captures the pains of the ill-treated soldiers and their helplessness: "Hah, if one were to worry about the injustices inflicted on us little men, the war would have ended a long time ago". Umeh gets the message and sabotages the "revolution" in his new post.

Women are also casualties of the war as the story "An Escape" reveals. They become sex objects used to satisfy the insatiable taste of the morally sterile officers. According to Major Amah, women are meant to be used and discarded:

> There are certain women whose course it seems, to give pleasure. They come and go, scattering their thighs on hundred beds. When they come to me, I take them like palm wine and think little of the rightness or wrongness of my action. (73)

"The Last Battle" story is appropriately followed by "War in the Head", another story which further espouses the psychological effects of the victims of the war. Even after the war is ended, the people remain stigmatized as rebels. Military presence on the campus does not help matters. Every little sound is taken for a bombing, gun shot or an air raid. According to Ekene, one of the students on campus, "it is funny what the war has done to me the faintest sound makes me nervous. I wonder when this feeling will cease". The feeling did not cease as his friend on hearing "car on fire" thought there was an air raid and jumps out of the car killing himself. The narrator captures it thus:

> Quickly as the driver hurried to slow down the flying car, Anthony thinking that there was an air raid, grabbed the door, yanked it wide open and jumped out. At the same time, the edge of the door hit his legs, propelling him against the resistant wind, which hauled him down the tar, battering his skull against the hard ruthlessness of fate. (144)

"The Minister's Wife" though not a civil war tale, is a product of it. Violence now becomes the norm and thuggery becomes an integral part of the political process. Barrister Kenneth Eze tries to go against the norm and is killed at the end. But instead of lamenting his death, the reader sees in the Barrister the only hope for the future. He had told his wife who was encouraging him to hire the "political boys":

> There is nothing more to consider. To associate with thugs is to expose yourself to them, to make yourself vulnerable let them find other employers. I have no need of them. It is for the people to elect their leaders. We can't terrorize them in order to lead them. (19)

The story, "A Band of Amazons", explores the themes of racism and exploitation. It is the celebration of women who rise against the oppression of their husbands in the hands of the colonial masters. They declare: "You white people na thiefs, ... They give you money make you pay our husbands, but you chop the money finish. If you no return our husbands to us, we go show you that hot water fit kill tortoise" (53).

"Lumber" and "A Baby for Chief Bayo" also make interesting reading. While the former tells of the ordeal of an indigent African student struggling for survival in a racial society, the latter satirizes the moral sterility that is a common feature of a degenerate national elite.

A highpoint of the book is that, like all good collections, each story strikes a peculiar cord with the author exhibiting a mastery of his craft. According to Emmanuel Obiechina in the foreword:

> The stories... stand up very well to the rigorous requirement of the short story form. Each story is a neatly cut slice of experience vibrant with life and unified in design by art and narrative skill. Art

is presented as a simulacrum of reality. (iv-v)

Without doubt, like most artistic creations of his generation, Enekwe seeks to protest, expose, correct and possibly change the cultural pattern of his society. What is unclear is his choice of criticism of contemporary society from an individualist perspective. This is stressed so much that it is even stated on the blurb:

> There is hope for redemption, for regeneration through this dark tunnel of despair and destruction and the author projects this hope as subsisting in the continuously individual heroic sacrifices on behalf of the society.

The success of this perspective is debatable. In the "Minister's wife", Kenneth Eze, like the man in Ayi Kwei Armah's *The Beautiful Ones Are Not Yet Born*, finds himself alone in the struggle for a moral regeneration. He makes no impact as he is destroyed in the end. The corrupt still have their way. Obiechina comes to the author's defense in his statement that what he has done in the collection is not lying or cheating "as many bad contemporary story writers do when they push a facile sort of optimism that flies in the face of all evidence." But this position is not inviolable. Evidence abounds in history that societies have progressed not only through individual exploits but also more through the collective push of the people. In spite of the times, it is very important to rekindle the need for seminal mating of new hopes and dreams for a new social order and artists are supposed to be at the vanguard. However, *The Last Battle and Other Stories* makes an interesting reading and with the simplicity of its diction, readers of different grades will find it quite stimulating.

14

In Demolition of the Old Dance

Book: *Theories of Dance in Nigeria*
Author: Onuora Ossie Enekwe
Publisher: Afa Press
Reviewer: Peter Ezeh

THEORIES of Dance an argumentative survey of prominent views on Nigerian dance by the author of the path finding and more ambitious *Igbo Masks*, the first book to establish the theatrical relevance of this Nigerian traditional dramatic art using applicable intellectual parameters. In the present work, Onuora Enekwe gives examples drawn from all parts of the country: Ibwa War dance of the Ninzam of Kaduna State, the dance of Yoruba's Gelede ceremony, the Kalabari's Ekine dance in Rivers State, the Igbo's Nkpokiti, and so on. Enekwe aims to look at these dances from (to use the word of another critic) an Afrocentric point of view, the much discussed intellectual's answer to nationalism which observers of our postcolonial literature should now be familiar with.

Enekwe recalls the theory of Peggy Harper, a foreign teacher of Nigerian dance, in which she divided the dance types into two contrasting categories of theatrical and ethnic, and also attacks the classification. Before Harper, Walter Sorell had made a similar classification using the notions "folk" and "theatrical" in a full-length book with the self-explanatory name: *The Dance through the Ages* in which he examined the subject in a wider geographical and temporal scope. Enekwe, himself a university classroom dance teacher who is frequently consulted by professional groups, rejects these terms because of their apparent association with stereotype Western scholarship which views traditional non-Caucasian societies as primitive, in contrast with their own societies which they consider civilized. Such a view, he believes, has affected the analyses of foreign teachers of Nigerian dances and those they influence through writing or teaching, including some Nigerians. One instance where a producer of an NTA programme on dance in a Nigerian northern State followed the example of Harper's ethnic-versus-theatrical classification was cited.

Enekwe contends that Nigerian dance needs to be examined on its own rather than to just slot it into existing intellectual pigeonholes based on Western conventions. Predictably he rejects the application of the much debated art for art's sake notion on the dances he discusses. Nigerian dances are at once sources of entertainment and useful social tools. Copious examples of dances that serve ritual marital, physical training and other needs are cited from all over the country. To use the familiar expressions, fine arts and practical arts merge in the Nigerian dance. "Nigerian traditional dance... is "utilitarian in many ways", he posits (26).

Examples are cited from classical Greek to illustrate that such a state of affairs is not all together strange even in the West. Enekwe takes all that trouble in an effort to repudiate rival theories which hold that a dance cannot serve both social and aesthetic needs at once, or to use the danceologist's jargon, be both efficacious and theatrical.

Enekwe's little book is so rich for its size, and for a book printed here, it is a pleasant surprise for the largely meticulous job of the proofreaders.

Photographs are liberally used to drive some points home to readers. Smooth prose and clarity of expression, which Enekwe's previous works are known for, are present here in a larger measure. Expert avoidance of needless recondite jargons makes a work such as this the choice of both ordinary readers and initiates. A friend whom I lent my own copy used the Igbo jaw-breaking epithet for an active dwarf *Anukporonkunejuonu* (much in little) to describe it.

Some readers will certainly rate its treatment of this taxing subject incomplete, but one should also note that the work is an adaptation of Enekwe's seminar papers. Let's hope that this is just the beginning of a bigger task. In the present work, for instance, Enekwe is argumentative all the way, hardly definitional. He demolishes the old theoretical structures without completing a new one in their place. For such an enormously important new view of the Nigerian (nay African) dance as Enekwe advocates, a totally different theoretical framework is needed.

 Chat

15

Aesthetics of African Literature

A DISCOURSE WITH OSSIE ENEKWE

GMT Emezue

"WHEN I was in the university, most of our lecturers sounded as if we didn't have drama in Africa. Eventually when we started reading something by (Ruth) Finnegan who had done a lot of work in the area of African oral literature, many of the lecturers and scholars were repeating the same thing. I actually doubted what they were saying. When I got to the United States I came in contact with drama works from other parts of the world. I saw Japanese and Chinese drama. But above all (I saw) how drama was presented in Japanese culture for instance.

Furthermore I studied history of drama and I realised that my teachers were wrong in supposing that we don't have drama in Africa. They felt that the dances which were ritualistic in nature lacked dramatic impetus because they believed that ritual and theatre were opposed to each other. But this was only the Western concept of drama which does not pertain to other cultures..."
– *O. O. Enekwe*

Q: Pofessor, you are a renowned critic and scholar of dramatic literature, as well as a creative writer of several poems and fiction. I suppose it will be proper to set the mood of this interview with a rendition of one of your poems.

Ans: Alright. I will read from the collection *Broken Pot*s. The poem is "To a friend made and lost in the war" (In memory of Martin Utsu).

> God had saved you
> At Ihiala, Ozubulu
> And Eluama where you lay
> On the tracks of enemy guns.
> But a hungry driver
> And a tired truck
> Hauled you into a ditch
> In a thick bush.
> Blood oozed from your nose,
> Mouth and ears;
> And at a village hospital
> Where they nursed you
> "God may get tired
> Of saving me," you said
> To me, a smile on your lips
>
> Two days later
> Soviet bomber rockets
> Burst your belly
> And tore your intestine
> On the white sheet
> Of the hospital bed.
> They must have been
> They bore you weeping
> To another place
> And tried to stitch you,
>
> To keep your soul
> From escaping in the purple flow.
> But you had too many holes.
> So you died among strangers.
> We could not find you.
>
> We came too late to the morgue,
> Too late to see you buried.
> We could not tell
> From the many mounds
> Which was yours
> Since the grave diggers
> Had left for the weekend,
> After a tiring week.
> They must have let you drop
> Like a cargo in the hold of a ship.
> We could tell how tired
> They must have been
> from the half-covered pits.
>
> We could not have
> Dug you out for a better pit.
> We only wanted to identify you portion
> And stand over you awhile
> At least to prove to you
> That you had friends.

Q: Naturally, the question that should follow such a moving rendition is "who" or "what." Specifically, who was Martin Utsu and what was your relationship with him?

Ans: I was in the Biafran Army during the Nigeria-Biafra war. At that time I was in the Propaganda Section. Martin was from Ogoja, Itigidi, that is the present Northern Cross River. He was one of the men in the group I headed. There was this young girl from Akwa Ibom and she and Martin were to get married. We all used to interact, you know, just as people do until suddenly, Martin died. And that was that.

Q: I find the elegiac note quite powerful; it resonates rather strongly of the African dirge sentiment you explored in "The Story of a Ceylonese girl" which I studied extensively in my book where I had remarked on circumstances for philosophical reflection on the tragic phenomenon

(Emezue 110)

Ans: In fact the first time I realised the power that this poem had over people was at Columbia. My course mates and I used to present our poems to each other. One day when we were out on a boat trip. We were yet to set off and one of the girls from Ireland suddenly caught my hand and said: "This poem is powerful; each time I read it I cry. It is almost as if I could see the whole thing happening." There have been other instances where people remarked on the power of the poem. So since that time I realized that the poem is quite touching.

Q: Funso Aiyejina once described your poetry as belonging to the 'generation of broken promises' who formed the Odunke community of artists' with chap books 'Omabe' and 'The Muse' as means of expression. What was your relationship with these groups?

Ans: Well, I was never a member of Odunke group of artists. But many of their members were my friends. I supported their activities, but I was never a member. Around that time I was very busy I was appearing on television as guest artist at Ukonu's club along with Sunny Okosun. The rehearsals and performances kept me very busy.

Q: What would you think was your greatest influence in your writings? And apart from the war are there other factors that influenced your writing?

Ans: Yes. The war influenced my writing all right. But the fact was that I was writing long before the war. But with war experience something happened to me. For the first time I became more aware of life. I realized that life is precious and should be treasured. I realised that life should be valued. There were many wastes during that war and the human waste was the greatest. I began to perceive life in a different dimension. Also when I travelled outside the country, I became more aware of what was happening. I became exposed to things going on around the world. I read other writers like Pablo Neruda, Ibsen, etc. I also interacted with other writers like Amiri Baraka who was a close friend. So all these acted as sources of influence on my writings. For instance my other collection of poems *Marching to Kilimanjaro* reacts to other issues in Africa. The other one *Gentle Birds* is a collection of poems which could also be enjoyed by adults as well as children. I subtitled it 'for the young and young at heart' so I wrote it so that adults can enjoy it too (*Reads from the collection*).

Q: In an interview, you observed that 'it should be possible for the artist to create in such a way that the reader is able to participate in what the writer is talking about'. In the search for a functional aesthetic, can the choice of language limit or enhance the realism of his art?'

Ans: Of course, it can. The diction affects the work. I feel that a writer in his use of language should aim at how to reach his audience. Language should express the action. You allow the character to say what they want to say. You know you just present the character to the audience and the audience interacts and judges the character. You know the writer does not judge his characters for the audience.

Q: How then would you describe the readership in Nigeria?

Ans: Very poor. Nigerian readership is very poor. But then it appears the writings that go on reflect the quality of reading one has undergone. The youths can no longer pick up a book and read. They are not interested. They don't have the time to read. They only read just to pass exams and nothing more. This has seriously affected the type of leadership that we produce nowadays. I think it might also have something to do with teaching. I remember when I was in secondary school. We had one teacher Mr Hart, a very articulate man who taught us in those days. He used to read out lines/portions of the literature book for us in class. Through he told a lot of stories but the way he handled the teaching made us become every interested in the subject. For instance when we read *Treasure Island*. He would come to the class and read: "One stormy nights..." All these attempts laid emphasis on aesthetic aspects of the language.

Q: Have you had a cause to review your work for technical reasons?

Ans: No Em... I will just say that I enjoy reading many of my books. I also do a lot of editing on my works. I have poems that I wrote over ten years ago, which I have not yet published because I am still going through them. I am very careful before I present my work to the public. So far I have not received any such reactions.

Q: Unlike some other books based on Biafran experience, one has noticed an attempt to change names of characters in *Come Thunder* even when it is obvious that most of these events happened in Biafra.

Ans: Immediately after the war people didn't want to talk about Biafra. Long after the war, one of my classmates kept calling a 'rebel'. I told him that I was not a rebel. But I noticed that they were so concerned with what I was doing at school then. Apparently we were held in suspicion. I believe that the poor reception of some of my books in other parts of Nigeria is because of the ethnic differences in the country. Take for instance my book *Come Thunder*, when it was presented to ANA, they only gave me 'special mention'. But even that 'special mention' was done in a funny manner. Where my should be they put only 'Ossie' leaving off the surname. Under the column for Book Title, they wrote 'Come' only instead of 'Come Thunder'. But abroad many critics were talking about my short stories and poems. So in the long run, my experience has been that once something is about Biafra, the story or work will not be well received in Nigeria. So in a way, that was why I changed the names of the characters. Also, within fictional bounds with the change of name of characters and setting, I was free to stretch my imagination to any scope. If I had adhered to factual names, I would have felt constrained to stick to facts. So I believe the change served dual purposes.

Q: A reviewer of *Come Thunder* dismisses it as paying 'little attention to details of description' and what she calls 'lack of deftness' in portraying the characters in the book. Buchi Emecheta, at the turn of the century lamented that African novels are not real novels because they are not as voluminous as those found in Europe. To you what makes an African novel?

Ans: Well, in my own view, it is not the size that makes a work a novel *per se*. Let's take for example a very small novel by Hemmingway, *The Old man and the Sea*. This a very small book, but very heavily loaded. The European concept of novel will tell you about culture, about what somebody is wearing, the colour of shoes, eyes and so on. We have not developed that sense of elaborate details because the African by nature is not in the habit of elaborating and expatiating on things by giving unnecessary details. Some times we talk about social environment, interaction, and dialogue. I am aware of all these. And I believe that everything that was meant to be described in that novel was described. I don't think that review was justified. In fact I described everything in that book. I don't know what other details that should have been added that was not done. (Reads a detailed description of environment and action on page 38.) I wonder what other description I should have added here without belabouring the point. As I said earlier, I believe the west (of Nigeria) didn't like *Come Thunder*. I am not surprised at that kind of review.

Q: You just pointed out that our novels are culturally influenced. Does this make the African novel inferior to their foreign (bulky) counterparts?

Ans: No. As far as I am concerned, our novels are as good as any in the world. When I was growing up I didn't even like bulky novels. The aesthetic elements have nothing to do with size.

Q: What prompted the writing of *Igbo Masks: The Oneness of Ritual and Theatre*?

Ans: When I was in the university, most of our lecturers sounded as if we didn't have drama in Africa. Eventually when we started reading something by (Ruth) Finnegan who had done a lot of work in the area of African oral literature, many of the lecturers and scholars were repeating the same thing. I actually doubted what they were saying. When I got to the United States I came in contact with drama works from other parts of the world. I saw Japanese and Chinese drama. But above all how drama was presented in Japanese culture for instance. Further I studied history of drama and I realised that many of my teachers were wrong in supposing that we don't have drama in Africa. They felt that the dances which were ritualistic in nature lacked dramatic impetus because they believed that ritual and theatre were opposed to each other. But this is only the Western concept of drama which does not pertain to other cultures. By the time I went to the U.S. to do my doctorate, I spent a lot of time thinking about this. My special authors were Shaw, Steinberg, and O'Neil. In fact I thought I was going to write my thesis on Shakespeare. But because of the realisation I had concerning our own drama, I decided to research into this. When I went to my supervisor and told him that I was researching into Igbo Masks, he asked me 'What was that?' I told him that it was African Theatre. Initially he was doubtful if such a thing actually existed. Fortunately, around this time a group from Yale theatre advertised for papers in African Theatre and I sent in a piece which they published. In fact when I was taking the book to my supervisor, I was afraid because I was not sure what his reaction would be. But he was excited and encouraged me. He was impressed. In fact what I am going to say now will buttress the point I made as far Yoruba and Igbo are concerned. Even in deciding to write on this Igbo theatre, I was sent to the department of Anthropology. The practice in Columbia then was that if a substantial part of your work falls into another discipline, a professor from that discipline will need to be part of your supervisory team. So they asked me to go and talk to a professor in the Department of Anthropology to see if he would join the team. I took it for granted that the professor would agree. But when I called him and told him "Prof, please I am writing my thesis on Igbo Masks," he said "Yes, I know you very well. What has that got to do with me?" and dropped the phone. I picked up the phone and called him again. He said "Are you taking my course in anthropology?" I said, "No." He dropped the phone again. Then in the evening a young Yoruba saw me and said that the Prof said he was in a bad mood when I called him. That I should call him again. But when I went to my supervisor he advised me to keep clear of the man. The man has already shown that he was prejudiced. So I had to find another prof, this time, a white and he was quite happy to supervise me. Eventually, when I finished writing, my supervisor had to cancel his leave to be present for my defence. It was during that occasion that it was decided that the work will be published. It was sent to the university press. The first reader praised the book highly. It was sent to the second reader who happened to be the same prof. His attack on the book was very personal. Eventually I had to abandon the idea of publishing the book abroad. Later I was told that Prof. Skimmer, the disgruntled prof, worked for Nigeria during the war and was anti-Igbo. He didn't want to hear anything concerning the Igbo.

But another interesting incident happened during the publication of the book at home. The manuscript was sent to Prof. Adedeji, the oldest professor in drama. He said that the status of the book was marginally acceptable. But by the time he was making this recommendation, the book had been accepted for publication by the *Nigeria Magazine*. He recommended the book reluctantly and also recommended that I should be marginally promoted. I didn't know what was happening at that time. But the University of Nigeria policy is that alternative opinion be sought when there is an unfavourable recommendation. From Prof Adedeji's recommendation he was saying that he was not sure whether *Nigeria Magazine* would publish the book. It was only later that the faculty discarded his recommendation and asked another professor's opinion. And this Professor gave high scores. But Prof Adedeji had not scored me for that book and I wondered why. It was much later when the editor of the *Nigeria Magazine* saw me that I got to know what was happening. I didn't even ask before he blurted out about how Prof. Adedeji had come to query them why they should accept my manuscript for publication. He told them that he was the oldest professor in theatre arts and he had a number of papers for publication too. "Please accept my papers" he had said. But the editor told him that his request could not be granted. The prof kept phoning and later took his complaint to the director of the publishing house. The director said to the editor: "Prof Adedeji is the oldest professor in theatre arts. Why do you not want to accept his papers?' The editor replied" "It is not that we do not want to accept it, but we already have our budget covered." At that time they had agreed that they would accept one work from North, West and East respectively. So they had no choice but to publish the book. Otherwise they would have killed *Igbo Mask*s. So that is how the fight has been. They have been fighting the book, but unfortunately the more they fight, the more popular the book becomes. They have been fighting *Come Thunder* too. Because you know that in *Companion to African Literature* edited by Douglas Killam and Ruth Rowe, *Come Thunder* is mentioned there. Under the section "West Africa" (Prof Enekwe reads) '...like the poetry, the prose explores various themes without showing any radical ideological or technical inclination by the writers. Igbo writers explore such issues as the anti-Igbo pogrom in Northern and Western Nigeria the direct cause of Biafran secession, Biafra's heroism... post war rehabilitation. Representative examples are S. O. Mezu's *Behind the Rising Su*n, Chinua Achebe's *Girls at Wa*r, ANC Aniebo's *Anonymity of Sacrific*e, John Munonye's *A Wreath for the Maiden*s, Flora Nwapa's *Never Agai*n, Buchi Emecheta's *Destination Biafr*a, Cyprian Ekwensi's *Survive the Peace* and

*Divided we Stan*d. Ossie Enekwe's *Come Thunder* is a book in the manner of Thomas Paine's *The Red Badge of Courage*' (end of reading). You know that *Red Badge of Courage* is a very short novel but very powerful. He compares *Come Thunder* with *Red Badge of Courage*. When I saw this I was happy because *Red Badge of Courage* also inspired me in writing my novels.

Q: Your book has indeed triggered off waves of similar explorations in other cultures like Ibitokun's *Dance as Ritual Drama and Entertainment in the Gelede of Ketu-Yoruba sub group of West Afric*a. Coming back to the idea of masking, I will like to put back to you the question you asked at the end of *Igbo Masks* but in this way: What has been the experience of Igbo Masking and theatre in the face of prostitutionalised entertainment?

Ans: Let's start with our Ivory Tower. Our so-called intellectuals are so obsessed with perpetuating European forms. They don't understand that these have very drastic and dangerous effect on everyone, for the fact that you are not promoting your own drama tradition. So the unfortunate thing now is that the young ones are growing up not knowing that there are indigenous forms that can compete with European forms. They believe that the only form that is really worthy of attention is the European form. Because even your colleagues don't seem to understand what you are talking about. They see it as an intellectual matter. They don't see it in terms of promoting indigenous drama which has the potential of bringing wealth to the country. I mean if you start a very good traditional performance group, it can bring in tourism. There was a time we started masquerade performance in the old Anambra State. I was a member of that committee. There is a video of most of the performances and at the beginning, it was very successful. But our academics feel differently. They feel that performance is just something for the paper. You put it there and it ends. But it is something that is meant to be practised regularly. We are not saying that we should have the same religion as our grandfathers. We don't have to have the same religion. But the mask, the idea of mask is quite universal. This *Adamma* and her daughter going around for instance. I used to tell my students that if we get just one *Adamma* mask and her daughter (also masked) without doing anything but just walking in from the university gate, you know just walking. You will just have people following them. That is the way tradition and culture is. And if we follow drama based on masking, a lot of people will understand it. Even in my department, I just noticed that most of the courses assigned to me were in the area of African Drama, as if that was the only thing I read in the university. The others want to be identified with foreign things. But I am not bothered. I believe that this concept of drama could even be realised in the 'written' form. I did a play called "Dance of Restoration." Where I wrote it was in the United States when I was a scholar in residence. I see it is pure African Drama, full of dance. Even the rhythm expresses Africa. We performed it at Shell Camp, Warri, when they invited us. Unfortunately I have not had time to complete it as fully as I would like. I saw it as an example of modern African Drama where you have characters dancing normally as they dance. So that is the problem. What I would like to see is more and more people acting and reflecting African dramatic traditions like the Chinese drama. When you watch it you know that it truly reflects the culture and people it talks about.

Q: It is interesting to hear you mention another drama piece you worked on. I recall an interview published in *Weekend Concord* (1991) where you mentioned your drama piece, 'The Betrayal', which was enacted at University of Nigeria. In that interview, you tagged your creativity in the drama genre as an 'experimentation' which aims 'to achieve a situation in drama whereby the word and action become one.' How has this experiment been received?

Ans: What I mean is a drama where the character is not the author. It is not the character speaking the voice of the playwright, but the character speaking according to the nature of the performance. Not the playwright giving lectures through the character. Anything that is not connected with the action will be eliminated. It is not a law that a character must make long speeches. A character can just sigh. That will reflect exactly how he feels. I must also add that I was an actor. On one occasion a woman came from Britain and conducted an audition and I came out best. One of the things that struck them was that I wasn't talking much, unlike the other actors who were shouting and raising their voices to emphasise their anger. They were totally surprised. We were all given the same script and the people who had been performing in the Eastern Nigerian Theatre took the main roles. I came into it because I just said to myself 'let them allow me to do the role just once as they believed I was not relevant. We argued and argued and at last the young woman agreed. The script was the same and we were all meant to act the role. By the time I finished my act the white woman exclaimed: "Excellent!, Excellent!" From that time John Ekwere started taking me seriously. So when I came in to Biafra to join the force at Aba they said there was an information group being directed by John Ekwere. I told him to help me get into the group. He said "Look, that's a waste of talent." This is because he had discovered that I was a good actor. He sent me back to the men in charge of the drama group. When I told the man that John wanted to see him, he asked "For what?" I told him that it was because I wanted to join the drama group. The man refused. So I went back to John Ekwere and told him what happened. John Ekwere was very angry with me. He said "What is wrong with you. Why did you tell him that it was about you?" But I had to tell the man the truth because I find it difficult to tell lies. That was how I lost out. I couldn't get into the drama group. But this is just to show you that some people were aware I had the talent for acting. In fact when I watch what is going on in the video film home movies nowadays), I am ashamed I don't even want to watch what they are acting. The actor doesn't need to talk too much. In normal life you don't need to talk too much. Sometimes somebody says something you don't respond. It is even more dangerous. It shows more anger when you don't respond. But our people believe that when you shout it shows you are very angry. Of course *Betrayal* is not yet complete. It is one of the works that I am still trying to expand and get published. But essentially it is talking about corruption which has become one of the main issues in Nigeria today.

Q: You have partly answered the next question we have concerning your view in the recent proliferation of home video in Nigeria today. The impact of this new wave of entertainment in the development of our socio-economic values as a nation...

Ans: The problem is diverse. I won't blame the people who are doing this because of the inactivity of the so-called intellectuals. It seems that the kind of education we are given makes us more educated but more inactive. So if you look around most of the businesses are run by people who are not educated. Even in politics, people who are there are mostly illiterates. Because the educated ones, once they have finished, they pick up these white-collar jobs, sit around and imitate Europeans. So talking about people being practical with things, if you want to be a performer, you perform. Don't feel that because you are a university lecturer, you cannot go on stage. So coming what these people (home video practitioners) are doing...well, there is vacancy, there is lack of performance, nothing is happening, so they are filling a gap. And they are there now and it is difficult for you to penetrate. Very difficult because the government is not interested. It is a very serious problem because they are transmitting a lot of wrong things that will take centuries to undo.

Q: Even our neighbouring countries, the way they perceive us because of this home video...

Ans: You see there is a lot of discrimination. Sorry to say that my experience has shown me that. I have done my best. When I started off I did my best. I formed a theatre group which I took round the schools in the East. We even performed in Umuahia. We went to Government College Umuahia where we did Macbeth. Do you remember those public performance of Macbeth in the 80s?

Q: Yes.

Ans: I was there. I took the plays even to Owerri and Port Harcourt. We went to perform in secondary schools. Sometime, in 1984, I did *Trial of Dedan Kimath*i. That was the first theatre production in the city of Abuja. Very successful production. But the press refused to talk about that production. That is what I mean by discrimination. Because if that production had been done by Yoruba performers, perhaps the news would have been everywhere. See, in 1993, I came back from United States of America and decided to take Nkpokiti dancers to the U.S. Before I returned to Nigeria, I had concluded with Brooklyn Academy of Music to sponsor the trip. Every thing worked out well. I even wrote a brochure which was the last thing they expected me to do. But just when we were about to start off, some Yoruba took over. When we now got the letter from this people they said that our performance will only be in New York. But before then we had agreed that we would tour American cities. But you are dealing with people who don't understand the power of culture. Most Igbo don't understand the power of culture. So you are alone when you are talking about culture because you are inadequate. Unless you talk about modernity.

Q: Your directing of Ngugi Wa'Thiongo's *Trial of Dedan Kimathi* performed at University of Nigeria and University of Ibadan was highly praised by Ihekweazu and Osundare. In an interview you said that the director could be a creator.

Ans: Yes.

Q: How has this concept helped your stage directing and how do you think it will help the concept of directing in Nigerian theatre?

Ans: It boils down to what I was talking about indigenisation of culture. Somehow when somebody is creating, the person is reflecting his culture, and the person is also reflecting himself. So somebody writes a play. That he writes a play does not mean that when you put it on stage it is going to be the same. In fact the play as written is different from the play on stage. That's the first assumption. Now, talking of culture, your culture, your cultural awareness should help you to determine the kind of staging; the

shape you give to a production, a piece of drama. You know what your people like and what they don't like. I think that's where the creativity of the director comes in. You begin to adjust the work in such a way that your audience becomes satisfied. Not just to pick the work and put it exactly the way the author puts it. What I did in *Trial of Dedan Kimathi* was to move things around. I took one of the last scenes forward. At the end of such changes I noticed that the audience enjoyed the performance very much.

Q: If you were directing *Death and the King's Horseman* with Wole Soyinka's pontification that no attempt should be made to make the play look like a clash of culture, can this be realised with that specific instruction?

Ans: It is his business to write a play as a playwright. He cannot pontificate for a director. If I take that play now and decide that instead of it being a Yoruba dance, it should be Igbo dance, he cannot stop it, eh? To the question of clash of culture and all that, of course there is clash of culture. Soyinka is a problem in that sense. For instance, when some Africans were talking of Negritude, Soyinka condemned Negritude. But Negritude was important. It was important because if you don't say "you are," nobody will say "thou art." This idea of saying that you are something is being carried out by Europeans all the time. So I disagree with Wole Soyinka in many areas. I think he is a powerful individual. But the danger comes when somebody starts to pontificate that this is the way things are. If you know the way, you think along that line but also you should allow other people to think in their own way.

Q: Let's look at *The Last Battle and other Stories*. Some critics had noted what they termed 'superficial treatment of female characters' in this book. It can be observed that your female characters are either depicted as being helpless, suffering, or being cheated and exploited by the men. And when they gear up to retaliate, they seem to shoot at the wrong target, like what happened in 'A Band of Amazons.' Does this reflect the Nigerian society or is it your own attitude or perception of women?

Ans: My own attitude to our women folk is that I recognise that they are exploited and I think in these works I merely draw attention to the fact that women are exploited. That is my main concern. And the way they end is not meant to be all that conclusive. It is a way of raising some questions. But saying the treatment is superficial (laughs) ... we are talking about a specific period. What was the one you mentioned?

Q: 'Emente' and 'A Band of Amazons.'

Ans: That is a way of emphasising the contradictions in the society. There is so much uncertainty. There is this other one where the girl jumps out of a moving car...

Q: 'Escape.'

Ans: Yes. I am trying to emphasize the vulnerability of women. I am emphasizing their humanity. The story 'Emente' is a unique short story. It was based on an actual experience and then I developed it. I don't think the case of Emente has anything to do with attitude of society. It has to do with ethnic factor because she was not Igbo; she was Efik and suddenly found herself abandoned in the hospital with nobody to attend to her. And in my youth, by that time I was about to enter the university. I had gone to see a doctor when I saw this lady. She had the Women Teachers College uniform. She walked into the place and she was collapsing. Eventually, they took her in to see the doctor. And I was curious; that type of curiosity that any young person would experience. So afterwards I wanted to find out whether she was okay. When I got there I was touched because the moment she started telling me about her condition, her helplessness, I could no longer escape. I could not abandon her. So I went to the hospital on some occasions to visit. I think I contributed to her survival because what happened, I had come to her and her mouth was closing. She told me that she had not eaten anything so I went to the gate of the hospital, where they have UNTH now and bought some eggs and then sliced the eggs and put into her mouth. So she was able to get something into her system. And before I left, the way she talked meant that she needed me there. She didn't want to be abandoned. She wanted somebody who cared to be close to her. I didn't know her, I didn't even know her name. So eventually I would go home and say 'I won't go to see her again.' But eventually my conscience would not allow me to rest. Then I would make ready and go see her. Then one day I went, only to discover that she had been discharged. Now if you wrote a story and concluded it with "She had been discharged," I mean, it won't have the impact. I continued working on it, whether it should be first person or second person. Whether I should be saying 'This young man did …' or whether it should be 'I'. And then how should it end? I wanted it to end without saying whether she was alive or dead. That would be more dramatic. And that was what I did.

Q: Yes, most of the stories in that collection ended that way. For instance 'Handling the Enemy' and 'The Last Battle...' Even in *Come Thunder,* you are not told whether the hero survives or not. At the last scene Emeka is just charging and charging...

Ans: You are very perceptive. It is just a question of your aesthetic sense.

Q: Your instinct as a dramatist must have aided your writings...

Ans: Of course it did. For instance, as I was saying about Emente, I did not see her as often as I used to before she was discharged. I think what happened was that I was afraid she was going to die. I was almost scared. But one day when I was in the university, we had a big party. That time we used to invite bands from Ghana such as the Uhuru Dance Band to come and play there. That was when the students union was better organised and run by responsible people. So I was sitting with my friends during the party when someone came over to me and said a lady wanted to see me. I walked over to the table and the young woman standing there. She said: 'Do you recognise me?' I looked at her and shook my head. She now said: 'do you remember the girl that you helped at....?' I shouted in surprise. Indeed it was the girl at the hospital. Now I was thinking of a name to give her in the book, I decided on 'Emente' because I believe the name will suggest someone from that area of Cross River. Not that this was her name, because I had forgotten her name. But I was happy that she survived. I believe I played a role in her survival because if I hadn't been there, who knows. Even my presence, even just visiting her must have helped her to survive.

Q: One also notices that most titles in that collection are ironical. For instance, in 'Escape' the heroine, instead of actually being free to live her life, 'escaped' into death' by jumping out of a moving car. Once again, 'The Last Battle' turns out to be the point of surrender for a very tough soldier...

Ans: (Laughs) ... Yes. The man surrenders. It is ironical alright.

Q: I wonder why the titles are like that. Does it point to some kind of artistic cynicism?

Ans: I think life is ironical. And irony is an artistic device, a powerful device because that is what the audience is never expecting.

Q: A few years ago Chinua Achebe felt that his role as an artist was to inform and educate his people. Whoever reads Achebe's works will come up with that sense of African pride and belonging. What would you like your readers to deduce from your works?

Ans: I think I am very much concerned with the issue of justice. If you read *Marching to Kilimanjaro* you will see this. I am a combatant and at the same time I feel deeply and this has an impact on my writing. Like some of those poems like "To a friend made and lost in the War," I couldn't have written it if I was not feeling deeply about the issue. And "The Story of a Ceylonese Girl" and there are other elegies. I wrote one 'To the memory of Nnabuenyi Ugonna." I wrote this poem 'In memory of Bernard Beckerman.' He was my supervisor in Columbia University. He died three years after I got my Ph.D. It was very painful because he took me like his son. So it was a way of expressing my love for the man. (Reads from the poem)

Gather the past about the bosom
Cast in the breeze of bronze
In cups of honey ...

It is the same poem that they published in the anthology that was put together for the man.

Q: Finally, let's look at your most recent book *Trails in the Mines* published 2000 by Minaj. This book is supposed to be a biography of Edmund Nwasike, the first Nigerian mining engineer and the first indigenous general manager of Nigerian Coal Corporation. But this book achieves more than this to become a documentation of early history of Nigerian Coal Corporation and social life in Enugu. Why did you adopt this style of writing?

Ans: Yes, as you have noticed, I went to great extent to show the socio-historical background of the events that occurred. How the colonial powers took over and the resistance they had from the various communities. And also to show the contradictions in the policy of the British. So I thought that it is not just enough writing a biography without showing the historical milieu in which most of the events took place. Most of the time I tried to capture the social background. That means that I had to do a lot of research to familiarise myself with that period. You know, instead of just writing a biography and just talking about the man because I know that one won't just understand the person without understanding the social milieu.

Q: In *Trails of Mines*, I noticed that the story centred on coal mines. Could that be a source for another story 'A Band of Amazons?'

Ans: Well, yes. It was like an echo from 'A Band of Amazons' helped in *Trail of Mines*. People then were much more aggressive than what we have now. Because people now are more docile. Very docile. Nigerians are more docile now unlike in those days. Because I remember. You know some of the things you remember, as a child will come into your stories whenever you find you are writing. When I was a little boy I saw women marching in protest. I experienced it. It became a way of keeping all that memories alive. Recollecting that incident when writing, the topic was so strong that it kept coming and the result is this 'Amazon'.

Q: Prof, what, briefly, can you tell us about yourself that brings to bear on your writings?

Ans: I don't know where to start with myself. But let me say this, when I was a child, I fought a lot. I fought. I wasn't fighting with my sibling. I fought outside the house. I fought not because I wanted something from people, but I fought whenever my right was denied me. For instance, when I was a child, I was very tiny and I found myself going to fetch water because Coal camp had no water that time. I would go with my bucket to fetch water at the pump. I found that very often bigger boys maltreated me. One day I brought my bucket. It was my turn to fetch water. We had to line up. So I took my bucket and put at the tap. Somebody bigger than I took my bucket and threw it away. Not just even pushing out my bucket, but he grabbed the bucket and threw it away. Then he ran. I was a good marksman. If I aimed a stone at someone, there is no escape. So as he was running, I picked a stone, aimed at his head, and threw. It hit him and blood started running. And some people started pursuing me, trying to catch me. I ran and ran. I didn't want them to take me to my father, because I was afraid my father would beat me for what I did. I knew that though I was fighting for my right, I had broken somebody's head in the process so I ran away. They took the young man to the hospital. Eventually the family of the boy came to our house and the matter was settled. Another day when I was in primary school, we were doing this 'show me your whip.' You know what 'show me your whip' means?

Q: Yes. You agree with your partner that both of you must always carry a whip and when you don't show yours, you will be flogged.

Ans: Yes. So one day, I had my whip and this person came to me. He was taller and bigger than I was. He said 'show me your whip.' I showed him my whip. He snatched it from me, flogged me, and started running. I looked around, found a piece of stone, and threw it at him. *Kpo-o*-o! If you saw the blood coming out of his head, it was like a stream. The young man got a big stone and started pursuing me. I ran into Uwani and a woman was carrying oil with basket on her heard. I got the woman and turned her around as I ran around her. As I tried to escape, the oil fell on the street and the boy missed me. But they caught the boy. The blood was flowing too much out of his head. So people caught him and stopped the blood. And my teacher said: *"I gbu go nu ya nu, I ga akpo ya eje hospital."* (You have killed him. You have to take him to the hospital.) So I took the boy to the hospital.

On another occasion, I was playing the masquerade. I was very tiny then but they used to call me 'Ossie Terror'. I was in front of the group. They were playing this ogene. You know, the ogene can make you do unimaginable superhuman things. So we were moving and there was this young man on the road. He refused to run like the others, because when the masquerade was coming you were supposed to give way. But he stood there. Heh! Then I said (there were certain incantations that we used to recite that goes like this):

I na echem? I na echem?
Nkiri, nkiri ka-ana ekiri mmanwu
Ukwu ose anaghi ari ya elu.
(Translation)
Are you still there? Waiting for me?
You can only watch a masquerade (from a distance)
You never climb the pepper tree

After reciting this, I turned around to give time so that the young man would go away. My group was following me playing their ogene. Then when we turned back he was still standing where he was. And I said "I na echem eche?" I walked straight up to him and flogged him. In short we beat him up thoroughly. As this was going on, the police came and arrested all of us. That was during Christmas. They took us to that police station near the near the market. They asked us: 'what went wrong?' We explained and at the end, they discharged us. That was one case.

In another direction, when I was a child, I had a good voice. At 11 years old, I was a member of the Holy Ghost Choir. We went to the Marian conference. At that age I could read music very well. Our choir master then was Reverend Fr. Kelly, a white man. That one passed and I went into St Patrick's choir. I eventually joined 'Young Voices' of Radio Nigeria. I was being paid some money. I was very busy, very active. I was even in the Boy's Scout. My mother would tell you I was always leading people who were bigger and older than I was. So even before she died she always said I sang beautifully, and people loved me for my voice. In my secondary school one of my teachers wanted to take me abroad. But I was afraid this might upset my family. So I didn't allow him to see my father.

Q: You were clearly a rebel of all sorts...

Ans: Essentially, you might say that I am a rebel because if there was an injustice, I would fight for the affected group. When I served in present Akwa Ibom sector as a ranger some Igbo soldiers from Aba were going there to kill the people. They would go in lorries to kill the people under the pretence that they were saboteurs. The Ngwa-Aba people would just go and ravage the areas. One of the tasks I was given was to protect the Akwa Ibom neighbours. We were based in Onicha-Ngwa from where we went into the town in Akwa Ibom. When we got to there we discovered that they had all fled into the bush. We searched until we saw a headless corpse. We laid ambush until one person came. He ran and we chased him into the bush. When we got there we saw the whole town inside the bush. I said to them "Ikot Inene is your town, those who said they are fighting the saboteurs were not sent by government. You have a responsibility to come back and defend your town. If any person comes to attack you, kill him." I ordered that they mount check points which they did. And they stopped being victims of the cowards that murdered them. That was how we ended the terror of the Aba Ngwa-Igbo. After I dealt with the people of Aba, they were saying that they didn't know that a fellow Igbo would deal with them that way.

So wherever there is injustice, I will fight against it. That is the way I was brought up. We had no strangers in our house. Everybody was the same. My creativity is highly influenced by this way of life.

THE END

WORKS CITED

Adeniji, Olayiwola. "'The Marks of Carnage': A Review of The Last Battle and other Stories." *The Guardian*, 29/7/ 1996.

Adimeba, Don. "'Enekwe's *Broken Pots* is here at last': A Review." *The Guardian*, 3/11/1986.

Ajao, Toyin. "Come Thunder: Another perspective of the civil War." *The Guardian*, 14/9/1985.

Ajayi, Sesan. "Of Faith not Broken." *The Guardian*. 3/12/1989.

Ajibade, Kunle. "The Compassionate Story of Onuora Enekwe the 48 year-old Nigerian Poet." *African Concord*. 6/5/1991.

– – –. "'I would have ended up a Musician': An Interview with O.O. Enekwe." *Weekend Concord*. 18/5/1991.

Ayejina, Funso. "The Poetry of Enekwe and Udechukwu: Two of a Kind." *The Guardian*. 19/4/1986.

Chiazo, Chi and Chukwuemeka Agbayi. "The Colour of Writing." *The Guardian*. 6/7/1998.

Emezue, GMT. *Comparative Studies in African Dirge Poetry*. AI: Handel Books, 2001.

Ezeh P. J. "A Guitar boy's Metamorphosis." *The Post Express*. 26/9/1998.

Ihekweazu, Edith. "Triumph of a Hero: Ngugi's play at UNN Convocation." *Times Union*. 16/2/1978.

Ikwuemesi, Krydz C. "Heroes and Songs - An Introduction to a Commemorative Exhibition on Ossie Enekwe." *Sunday Vanguard*. 14/6/1998.

Ohaeto, Ezenwa. "Art Personality: Ossie Enekwe." *Daily Times*. 27/4/1991.

Osundare, Niyi. "The Fighting Spirit" (Review of presentation of Kimathi at Unibadan.) *West Africa*. 14/4/1984.